Gastric Sleeve Bariatric Cookbook

BECCA RUSSELL

D1708160

© Copyright 2022 - All rights reserved.

This document is aimed at providing accurate and reliable information regarding the subject at hand. The publication is sold because the publisher is not obligated to provide qualified, officially permitted or otherwise accountable services. If any advice is necessary, whether legal or professional, it should be ordered from a person with experience in the profession.

In no way is it legal to reproduce, duplicate, or transmit any part of this document in either electronic means or printed format. Recording of this publication is strictly prohibited and any storage of this document is not allowed unless with written permission from the publisher.

TABLE OF CONTENTS

TABLE OF CONTENTS

TABLE OF CONTENTS

TABLE OF CONTENTS

INTRODUCTION

How would you like to lose 70% of your body weight in just 12 months?

It may sound crazy, but every year more than 150,000 people in America take advantage of this procedure and see the fat disappear from their bodies...

... even if they had previously tried all kinds of workouts or diets, with poor results.

It is not science fiction, but one of the great breakthroughs of modern medicine.

Wondering what this is all about?

Sleeve gastrectomy – one of the most effective procedures for weight loss, with a success rate approaching 90%.

But that's not all.

As a matter of fact, you ought to be told that this particular surgery won't just help you shed excess pounds.

According to a study published in the National Library of Medicine, bariatric surgery patients also see their risk of cardiovascular disease drop by 42%...

... on top of a 30% decline in all-cause mortality.

Therefore, not only will you see your body shape- up, but at the same time, the quality of your life will improve dramatically.

However, there is one important aspect you need to take into account.

In terms of weight loss, 90% of people see their accomplishments fade within 5 years.

This means that 9 out of 10 people regain the pounds they lost – and some.

You see, weight loss is a long-term game.

Surgery alone cannot ensure that you achieve your goals.

This is why doctors recommend combining bariatric surgery with a controlled diet and a healthy lifestyle.

It can be a daunting task and that is why many people fail.

Boring diet...

... always the same foods...

... eating only out of necessity and no longer for enjoyment.

However, today I am here to make this task easier for you...

... and to make sure that you are part of the 10% of people who enjoy long-term results.

This is why I have compiled 1,000 days' worth of tasty recipes to help you lose weight healthily and consistently.

And all that without sacrificing the pleasure of eating or completely disrupting your diet.

But first, let me explain what bariatric surgery is and share the healthy habits to reduce the risks associated with the operation, as well as the dietary strategies to adopt before and after the procedure...

... so you can reduce the risks associated with this surgical procedure while reaping all its benefits.

Are you ready?

Great, let's get started.

1. Bariatric surgery: risks and benefits

In this first section, I want to show you the 3 types of weight loss surgeries most commonly practiced in America.

I will also disclose the advantages and disadvantages of the different approaches.

First, however, you need to know that in order to undergo these surgeries, you must meet certain requirements.

Among them:

- Having a body mass index equal to, or greater than, 40;
- Having a body mass index between 30 and 39, coupled with a condition such as Type 2 diabetes or hypertension;
- Having already tried to lose weight with other approaches in the past;
- Being prepared to lead a healthy lifestyle in the long term.

Indeed, as I mentioned earlier, correct nutrition and lifestyle are crucial to maintaining the results attained through surgery.

Now I will tell you about the 3 most common types of weight loss surgery in America.

Let's start with the first one.

1. Gastric bypass

In this procedure, the surgeon divides the stomach into two parts – one larger and one smaller.

As a result, a small pouch is created that the surgeon connects directly to the small intestine.

Finally, a new connection between the stomach and the intestine is also created, so that the enzymes can digest the food.

Therefore, when you ingest food, it will pass into the small stomach pouch and go directly into the intestine.

Besides absorbing fewer calories, you will feel full faster.

A 2018 study showed that gastric bypass is the type of weight loss surgery that has more complications.

Let me now explain the advantages and disadvantages of this approach.

Pros	Cons
• Greater weight loss than with gastric bandage • No foreign object in the body	• Hard to reverse • Higher likelihood of vitamin and iron deficiencies than with gastric band or gastric sleeve • Higher likelihood of surgery-related problems than with gastric band • Increased risk of alcohol consumption disorders

2. Adjustable gastric band

In this procedure, the surgeon places an adjustable band around your stomach.

The band then divides the organ into two sections: an upper and a lower one.

The two parts are connected by a narrow passage, regulated by the band itself.

When you ingest food, it pools in the upper section of your stomach.

Then, in a slow and controlled manner, it transitions to the lower part.

That's why you will feel full faster.

The surgical procedure also involves inserting subcutaneous access, which will allow the surgeon to adjust the size of the band around your stomach.

Let me now explain the advantages and disadvantages of this approach.

Pros	Cons
• Can be adjusted and reversed • Brief hospital stay • Low risk of surgery-related problems • Does not affect the intestine • Lower risk of vitamin deficiency	• Smaller weight loss compared to other types of surgery • Frequent visits to adjust the band • Possible body intolerance to the band, requiring its removal

3. Sleeve gastrectomy

In this surgery, the surgeon removes about 80% of your stomach.

This approach also eliminates cells that produce a particular hormone: ghrelin.

This substance is responsible for appetite.

Therefore, as a result of removing these cells and reducing your stomach, you will feel less hungry and get full faster.

Here are the advantages and disadvantages of this procedure.

Pros	Cons
• Major weight loss • Shorter hospital stay • No changes to the intestine • No foreign body inserted	• It is irreversible • Possible vitamin and iron deficiency • Higher risk of complications compared to gastric banding • Risk of acid reflux and hiatal hernia

Compared with gastric bypass, sleeve gastrectomy may have fewer risks associated with the surgical procedure.

Therefore, it can be a valid choice if you have already tried to lose weight in the past, without great results.

Perhaps you have already undergone the surgery – or maybe you are planning to do so.

Either way, what results can you expect?

- 60-70% weight drop in the first year after surgery
- Decrease in excessive hunger
- Reduction or even remission of serious diseases, including:
- Hypertension
- High cholesterol
- Urinary incontinence
- Cancer
- Joint pain
- Asthma
- Hepatic steatosis
- Type 2 diabetes

Specifically, research shows that in 60-80% of cases, patients who underwent sleeve gastrectomy reduced or reversed their type 2 diabetes.

Still, you should be aware that weight control surgeries can increase the risk of vitamin deficiency and cause some inconveniences.

For this reason, it is crucial to lead a correct lifestyle and follow the right diet.

In the next section, I want to show you 4 healthy habits to reduce or prevent surgery-related issues and reap all the benefits of weight loss.

2. The 4 habits to make the procedure safer

Now I want to inform you of the problems that sleeve gastrectomy can cause – and how you can avoid or reduce them.

Whether you've already had the surgery or maybe you have it planned, these healthy habits will help you take proper care of your body.

Perhaps they will seem like obvious suggestions to you.

Nevertheless, doctors and researchers themselves continually recommend these steps simply because many people do not follow them.

Also these healthy habits will not only reduce or wipe the risks associated with surgery...

... but they will also help you prevent several diseases such as:

- Type 2 diabetes
- Hypertension
- Cancer
- And many more!

So, here are the 4 strategies that can help you counteract the potential problems of bariatric surgery.

1. Losing weight

Based on the latest data, about 70% of the American population is overweight.

But the most alarming fact is that mortality in obese people can also increase threefold – compared to a fit and well person.

If you have not yet undergone the surgery, following the right diet before the operation is very important.

Indeed, in 2015 a large-scale survey showed that among bariatric surgery patients, those who preemptively lost at least 9.5% of their body weight, faced a significantly lower risk of experiencing postoperative complications.

That's why in the next section I'll show you exactly how to set up your diet to prepare for surgery.

2. Exercise more

A sedentary lifestyle increases the risk of death from cardiovascular disease by 90%.

And, as you know, obese patients are intrinsically at higher risk of developing such conditions.

To begin with, the guidelines suggest engaging in physical activity for 30 minutes, 5 times weekly.

You won't need to start with hours of heavy workouts or run marathons.

Even a light walk can be a great starting point.

3. Quit smoking

According to a study published in the National Library of Medicine, smoking causes 30% of all cancers.

But that's not all.

In fact, smoking stimulates the immune response and increases inflammation, which is one of the underlying mechanisms of weight gain.

4. Follow a correct diet

Now, let's dive into the thick of it.

As I told you at the beginning, a proper diet makes all the difference in the results you can get from sleeve gastrectomy.

But more importantly, the right diet will help you counteract the deficiencies that can occur after such surgery.

In fact, as you ingest less food, your body may experience a shortage of some important nutrients, including:

- Vitamin A
- Vitamin B12
- Vitamin D
- Vitamin E
- Vitamin K
- Folic acid
- Calcium
- Iron

In particular, the deficiency of this important mineral iron, can result in a condition called anemia.

Anemia occurs when there are not enough red blood cells to carry enough oxygen to your cells.

As a study published in the National Library of Medicine shows, up to 49% of bariatric surgery patients develop anemia after the procedure.

In such cases, an appropriate diet can help you counteract the problem.

In addition, your doctor may also prescribe some supplements.

But that's not all.

In fact, calcium and vitamin D deficiency can increase the risk of osteoporosis.

In fact, a study published in PubMed in 2017 shows that the risk of bone fractures is 2.3 times higher in people who have undergone bariatric surgery than in individuals who have not.

Again, diet and supplements can make a difference.

This is exactly why I have decided to devote the next two sections to the eating strategies to adopt both pre- and post-surgery.

I will show you how to structure your diet and which foods to choose or avoid.

3. The pre-operative diet in 5 steps

In this section, I want to show you the 5 steps to best prepare for your bariatric surgery.

If you have already been through a surgery, you may want to skip to section no. 4 instead.

Section 4 is where I will explain how to best manage the post-operative phase and how to structure your diet to lose weight healthily and permanently.

But if you have not yet undergone surgery, then stick with me, because in this section you will find all the information you need to take proper care of your body ready for the procedure.

But first, let me show you the benefits of following these 5 steps before your surgery.

Make the procedure safer and easier. The pre-operative diet helps you dissolve any fat deposits around the liver, so the surgeon can operate with more space, given both you and them more peace of mind.

Reduce the risk of complications. Obesity can increase the risk of medical complications during and after surgery. Losing weight can therefore reduce this possibility.

Start creating the right habits. Once you are done with surgery, you'll already know how to eat healthily to take care of your body.

Those are the 3 main advantages of following the right pre-operative diet.

Now back to your preparation. As I mentioned before, this phase consists of 5 steps.

It's important to follow them in the right sequence, in order to show up for your surgery in the best possible condition.

Below I will show you each step in detail.

Plus I will also tell you which foods to choose – and which would be best avoided. Step 1: before the surgical procedure

At this stage, your main purpose should be to reduce calories and eat healthy and light foods.

The goal is to lose weight and make your surgery safer.

To accomplish this, you can adopt 4 strategies:

- Reduce carbohydrates. High-carb foods are often also high in calories. That's why you should reduce your intake. Plus a low-carb diet will help you stabilize your blood sugar levels more effectively.
- Eat the right proteins. Proteins help support your muscles and provide energy to your body. So try to have at least 60 grams worth of protein content per day.

- Introduce healthy fats. Healthy fats, like Omega-3s, are powerful allies of your heart. Besides reducing inflammation, they also help lower bad cholesterol and can protect you from cardiovascular disease.
- Stay hydrated. Remember to drink at least half a gallon (2 liters) of water per day to avoid dehydration.

At this stage, in your diet you can include foods like:

- Lean meats
- Chicken or turkey breast
- Lean cuts of beef or pork
- Fish. For example, cod, sea bream, or salmon
- Green vegetables such as spinach or salad
- Vegetables like broccoli, tomatoes, or peppers
- Good fats like extra virgin olive oil
- Fresh fruit such as berries, peaches, or oranges.

Meanwhile, you should avoid these foods:

- Fast food meals
- Packaged meals
- Fatty meat
- Processed meats like sausages
- Deep-fried foods
- Refined pasta and carbohydrates
- Fatty cheeses
- Alcohol
- Sugary drinks
- Sweets.

So, these are the recommendations for a correct diet to follow for at least 3 weeks before the operation. Remember to check with your doctor before making any dietary changes, just to check they are right for you.

Let's now move on to the next step.

Step 2: 2 weeks before surgery

At this stage, the same advice as the previous week still applies.

However, in some cases, since you may have been taking nutritional supplements to support you, your doctor may ask you to stop taking some supplements.

So, ask your doctor specifically about supplements.

Step 3: 1 week before surgery

Your doctor may now tell you to stop taking certain medications.

The aim is to reduce the risk of hemorrhage or any potential postoperative problems.

Again, your doctor will provide you with instructions specific to your situation.

Step 4: 2 days before surgery

At this point, your doctor may tell you to remove solid foods from your diet.

Obviously, the earlier advice still applies, therefore:

- No sodas or sugary beverages
- No alcohol
- No coffee.

The doctor will most likely advise you to have clear liquids such as broth, water and possibly protein shakes instead.

Step 5: the night before surgery.

In preparation for the surgery, typically you will also need to suspend any intake of liquid foods.

Indeed, on the day of surgery, your digestive tract should be empty.

This is because besides making the procedure itself safer, it will reduce the risk of post-operative complications.

As always, you must follow the advice of your doctor. I am simply explaining the typical steps so that you are aware of what may happen.

So, these are the 5 steps your doctor is likely to tell you to follow when preparing for bariatric surgery.

Now you're ready to move on to the last section, where I'm going to show you exactly how to set up your post-operative diet plan.

4. The 6 stages of the post-operative diet

So far we've seen how to structure your diet before surgery.

Now I want to show you how to take care of your body in the post-op phase.

I'll instruct you on how to set your diet, week by week.

I will also provide a list of foods to include in your diet – as well as those to avoid.

In this case, the strategy will consist of 6 steps.

However, you should be aware that these are general directions.

Depending on your specific situation, your doctor will tell you exactly how to organize your recovery process.

That said, Let's begin with the first step.

Step 1: 2 days after surgery

This is perhaps the most delicate stage.

Your body is beginning to recover from the operation, so you need to be very careful.

Therefore, just stick to ingesting clear liquids at room temperature, such as water.

Remember to steer clear of any sugary, carbonated, or caffeinated beverages.

Step 2: 3 to 7 days after surgery

After the first few days, your doctor may advise you to ingest some liquid foods.

These may be:

- Fat-free milk
- Soy drinks
- Broth.

But be sure to check with your doctor first.

Step 3: second week after surgery

After the first 7 days, you could also start adding some liquid, soft, and easily digested foods.

But keep in mind one very important aspect: you should eat in an extremely slow and controlled way.

Try chewing your food about 20 times, pausing between bites, and introducing small portions for each meal.

At this stage some possible foods – remember to check with your doctor – are:

- Protein shakes
- Creamed rice
- Fat-free yogurt and Greek yogurt
- Soups
- Fruit purée
- Sugar-free ice cream or pudding.

Avoid everything I didn't include in the previous list, but especially:

- Solid foods
- Sugary drinks
- Carbonated Drinks
- Caffeine

Step 4: third week after surgery

At this point, you can start reintroducing solid foods, albeit of a soft and easily digestible kind.

Always remember to have small portions at each meal and to chew at least 20 times per bite.

You should also avoid the consumption of salt or spices because they may irritate your stomach and digestive tract.

Some new foods to introduce could be:

- Eggs
- Beans
- Fish
- Lean minced meat
- Cooked vegetables
- Soft fruit
- Cottage cheese.

However, keep avoiding any other foods.

You should also continue to follow healthy habits including:

- Have no more than 3 main meals per day
- Limit snacking to 2 times a day
- Avoid fatty foods
- Avoid refined foods
- Consume at least 60 grams of protein per day
- Avoid fibrous foods such as asparagus or broccoli
- Avoid sugars
- Take vitamins or other supplements as per your doctor's advice.

Now, let's move on to the next step.

Step 5: first month after surgery

4 weeks have now gone by since you underwent surgery.

Your body starts to recover and find a new balance.

This is why you can also start introducing solid and more complex foods.

You can now add to your diet:

- Sweet Potatoes
- Well-cooked chicken
- Cereals without sugar
- Low-fat cheese
- Fruit.

However, for the time being, you should still avoid more complex foods, rich in carbohydrates or fats.

Here are some examples to avoid:

- Rice
- Pasta
- Bread
- Steak
- Processed meat

- Baked goods
- Sweets
- Fibrous vegetables
- Nuts.

Well, you're now ready to move on to the last step.

Step 6: fifth week after surgery and onwards

At this point, your body will have regained its balance.

Therefore, you may resume more of your normal diet.

However, you should be careful to avoid certain categories of foods, including:

- Fast food
- Processed meat like sausages
- French fries
- Deep-fried foods
- Sweets
- Foods high in fat
- Carbonated Drinks
- Sugary drinks
- Wholemilk-based foods.

The general rule is to avoid foods with "empty" calories.

Since your stomach will have a capacity of about 20% compared to before, you need to focus on a healthy diet rich in nutrients such as vitamins and minerals.

Start reintroducing one new food at a time, so you can test how your body reacts.

Remember to drink about half a gallon / 2 liters of water a day.

You can also reintroduce caffeine, albeit in moderation.

Continue to maintain a healthy lifestyle and consider starting some physical activity for 30 minutes a day, 5 days a week, if your doctor agrees.

From now on – if you follow the right diet and maintain a healthy lifestyle – you will continue to lose weight regularly.

Conclusion

We have now reached the end of this section.

I hope you now have a clearer idea of how to take proper care of your body both before and after bariatric surgery.

I showed you what are the various types of surgery and advantages and disadvantages of each procedure.

Then you learned the risks of these different approaches and 4 ways to mitigate them.

Finally, I offered a plan to organize your pre- and post-operative diet.

You are now ready to discover all the recipes I have collected for you.

Thanks to these recipes, you will be able to enjoy a different menu every day, for more than 1,000 days.

Wondering how that's possible?

It's very simple, just let me show you.

Picture having 4 delicious meals every day.

Now, let's divide the number of recipes by 4.

The result is 35+.

For each breakfast, lunch, snack, and dinner, you will have on average 35+ recipes to choose from.

This means that day in, day out, you can create a different menu by choosing for each of 4 meals one of the 35 dishes I have provided.

As you can imagine, the number of possible combinations is huge.

So, you will have a different menu combination to enjoy for over 1,000 days.

Now, I leave it to you to discover these tasty recipes, thanks to which you can take care of your own and your loved ones' bodies.

Chapter 1
BREAKFAST

1
Blueberry Protein Pancakes

 5 minutes   5 minutes   2

Ingredients

- 1 cup blueberries
- 3 eggs
- 1 ½ tbsp coconut oil, melted
- ½ cup whole wheat flour
- 2 tbsp vanilla protein powder
- non-stick spray, for cooking

Directions

1. Mix the eggs in a bowl.
2. Add the wheat flour, vanilla protein powder, coconut oil, and blueberries, and mix properly.
3. Now spray a non-stick pan.
4. Add some of the batter and cook on each side till the color turns light brown.
5. Your pancakes are ready to be served.

Nutrition: Calories: 358 kcal; Fats: 11 g; Carbohydrates: 34 g; Protein: 27 g

2
Cabbage and Coconut Chia Smoothie

 5 minutes   0 minutes   1

Ingredients

- ⅓ cup cabbage
- 1 cup cold coconut milk, unsweetened
- 1 tbsp chia seeds
- ½ cup cherries
- ½ cup spinach

Directions

1. Add coconut milk to your blender.
2. Cut cabbage and add to your blender.
3. Place chia seeds in a coffee grinder and grind to a powder.
4. Pour the powder into the blender.
5. Cut the cherries and add them to the blender.
6. Wash and dry the spinach and chop.
7. Add to the mix.
8. Cover and blend on low followed by medium power.
9. Check the texture and serve chilled!

Nutrition: Calories: 121 kcal; Fats: 6 g; Carbohydrates: 16 g; Protein: 2 g

3
Cheese-Filled Acorn Squash

 10 min   50 min   3

Ingredients

- 1 lb. tofu, firm
- 1 tsp basil
- 1 pinch black pepper, freshly ground
- 1 tsp onion, chopped finely
- 1 tsp garlic powder
- 1 cup cheddar cheese, reduced-fat, grated
- 2 pieces acorn squash, halved, seeded
- 1 cup celery, diced
- 1 cup mushrooms, fresh, sliced
- 1 tsp oregano
- ⅛ tsp salt
- 8 oz. tomato sauce

Directions

1. Pre-heat the oven to 350°F.
2. Arrange the acorn squash pieces, with their cut sides facing down, at the bottom of a glass dish.
3. Place in the microwave oven and cook for about twenty min or until softened.
4. Set aside.
5. Heat a saucepan (nonstick) on medium, then add the tofu (sliced into cubes).
6. Cook until browned before stirring in the onion and celery.
7. Cook for 2 min more or until the onion is translucent.
8. Add the mushrooms. Stir to combine and cook for an additional 2 to 3 min. Pour in the tomato sauce as well as the dry seasoning.
9. Give everything a good stir, then spoon equal portions of the mixture inside the acorn squash pieces.
10. Cover and place in the oven to cook for about fifteen min. Uncover and top with the cheese before returning to the oven. Cook for 5 more min or until the cheese is melted and bubbling.
11. Serve immediately.

Nutrition: Calories: 424 kcal; Fats: 21 g; Carbohydrates: 30 g; Protein: 26 g

4
Chilled Watermelon Smoothie

 **5 minutes**   **0 minutes**   **1**

Ingredients

- 1 cup watermelon chunks
- ½ cup coconut water
- 1 tbsp lime juice
- 4 mint leaves
- 4 ice cubes

Directions

1. Put all the ingredients in your blender and blend until smooth.
2. Serve chilled!

Nutrition: Calories: 72 kcal; Fats: 0 g; Carbohydrates: 16 g; Protein: 2 g

5
Choco Lovers Strawberry Shake

 10 minutes   **0 minutes**   **1**

Ingredients

- ½ cup heavy cream, liquid
- 1 tbsp cocoa powder
- 1 tbsp stevia
- ½ cup strawberry, sliced
- 1 tbsp coconut flakes, unsweetened
- 1 ½ cup water

Directions

1. Put all of the ingredients into a blender.
2. Blend until you have a smooth and creamy texture.
3. Serve chilled and enjoy!

Note: Consider this a special treat and do not consume more than 1 a week!

Nutrition: Calories: 513 kcal; Fats: 48 g; Carbohydrates: 118 g; Protein: 6 g

6
Delish Pineapple and Coconut Milk Smoothie

5 minutes | **0 minutes** | **1**

Ingredients

- ¼ cup pineapple, frozen
- ¾ cup coconut milk

Directions

1. Put the ingredients into a blender and blend well on high.
2. Once the mixture is smooth, pour the smoothie into a tall glass and serve.
3. Chill and enjoy!

Nutrition: Calories: 52 kcal; Fats: 4 g; Carbohydrates: 6 g; Protein: 0 g

7
Cinnamon Chiller

5 minutes   0 minutes   1

Ingredients

- 1 cup almond milk, unsweetened
- 2 tbsp vanilla protein powder
- ½ tsp cinnamon
- ¼ tsp vanilla extract
- 1 tbsp chia seeds
- 1 cup ice cubs

Directions

1. Put all of the ingredients into a blender.
2. Blend until you have a creamy texture.
3. Serve chilled and enjoy!

Nutrition: Calories: 179 kcal; Fats: 5 g; Carbohydrates: 8 g; Protein: 23 g

8
Ezekiel Bread French Toast

5 minutes   15 minutes   2

Ingredients

- 4 slices Ezekiel bread
- ½ cup coconut milk or unsweetened almond milk
- 2 eggs
- 2 tbsp coconut sugar
- 1 tsp vanilla
- 1 tsp Stevia
- Cinnamon, to taste

Directions

1. Combine all the ingredients (except for the Ezekiel bread) in a bowl.
2. Sink each slice of bread into the mixture.
3. Fry using a skillet for about 4 minutes on each side or until lightly browned.
4. Once cooked, serve with syrup.

Nutrition: Calories: 261 kcal; Fats: 7 g; Carbohydrates: 35 g; Protein: 15 g

9
Heart-Friendly Sweet Potato and Oats Waffles

5 minutes

10 minutes

2

Ingredients

FOR THE WAFFLES:
- 1 cup rolled oats
- ½ cup sweet potato, cooked and skin removed
- 1 whole egg
- 1 egg white
- 1 cup almond milk
- 1 tbsp honey
- 1 tbsp olive oil
- ¼ tsp baking powder
- ¼ tsp salt

FOR THE SERVINGS:
- Banana, sliced
- Maple syrup

Directions

1. Preheat a waffle iron.
2. Meanwhile, add all the ingredients to a blender and process until pureed. Let the mixture stand for 10 minutes.
3. Coat the waffle iron with a nonstick cooking spray.
4. Pour ⅓ cup of the batter into each mold. Cook for about 3–4 minutes per batch or 30 seconds longer after the light indicator turns green. Usually, waffles are done after the steam stops coming out of the waffle iron.
5. Serve with banana slices and maple syrup on top.

Nutrition: Calories: 322 kcal; Fats: 14 g; Carbohydrates: 37 g; Protein: 11 g

10
Hearty Alkaline Strawberry Summer Deluxe

5 minutes   0 minutes   1

Ingredients

- ½ cup organic strawberries/ blueberries
- ½ banana
- 2 cups coconut water
- ½-inch ginger
- Juice of 2 grapefruits

Directions

1. Add all the listed ingredients to your blender.
2. Blend until smooth.
3. Add a few ice cubes and serve the smoothie.
4. **Enjoy!**

Nutrition: Calories: 265 kcal; Fats: 1 g; Carbohydrates: 60 g; Protein: 6 g

11
Lemon Melon Popsicle

5 minutes   4 minutes   4

Ingredients

- 3 cups melon, chopped
- 1 tsp stevia
- 1 tsp fresh lemon juice

Directions

1. Put all the ingredients into the blender and blend until smooth.
2. Pour the melon mixture into the Popsicle molds.
3. Place in the refrigerator for 4 hours or until set.
4. Serve and enjoy.

Nutrition: Calories: 57 kcal; Fats: 0.25 g; Carbohydrates: 9 g; Protein: 1 g

12
Mango Pineapple Green Smoothie

3 minutes

0 minutes

2

Ingredients

- 1 cup mango chunks, frozen
- 1 cup pineapple chunks, frozen
- 1 cup fresh spinach or kale
- ¼ cup orange juice
- ½ cup non-fat plain or vanilla Greek yogurt
- 1 tbsp flaxseed, ground
- 1 tsp stevia, granulated

Directions

1. Put all of the ingredients in the pitcher of a blender. Purée until smooth.
2. Serve immediately.

Nutrition: Calories: 157 kcal; Fats: 0.5 g; Carbohydrates: 33 g; Protein: 6 g

13
Mango's Gone Haywire

5 minutes

0 minutes

2

Ingredients

- 1 mango, diced
- 2 bananas, diced
- 1–2 oranges, quartered
- Dash lemon juice
- 1 tbsp hemp seed
- ¼ tsp green powder
- Coconut water, as needed

Directions

1. Put orange quarters in the blender first, and blend.
2. Add the remaining ingredients and blend until smooth.
3. Add more coconut water to adjust the thickness.
4. Serve chilled!

Nutrition: Calories: 255 kcal; Fats: 5 g; Carbohydrates: 56 g; Protein: 6 g

14
Mint Orange Infused Water

 5 minutes   5 minutes   4

Ingredients

- 10 fresh mint leaves
- 4 cups water
- 1 apple, sliced
- ½ cup of grapes
- 1 orange, sliced

Directions

1. Put the grapes, sliced orange, apple and mint leaves in a glass jar.
2. Pour water into the jar and stir well.
3. Place the jar in the refrigerator for 1 hour.
4. Serve and enjoy.

Nutrition: Calories: 55 kcal; Fats: 0 g; Carbohydrates: 14 g; Protein: 1 g

15
Raspberry Popsicle

 5 minutes   5 minutes   3

Ingredients

- 4 cups of raspberries, frozen
- 1 tsp stevia
- 1 ½ cup fresh grapefruit juice

Directions

1. Add all the ingredients to the blender and blend until smooth.
2. Pour raspberry mixture into the Popsicle molds and place in the refrigerator for 3–4 hours.
3. Serve and enjoy.

Nutrition: Calories: 134 kcal; Fats: 1.3 g; Carbohydrates: 30 g; Protein: 2.6 g

16
Refreshing Strawberry Limeade

 5 minutes   5 minutes   1

Ingredients

- ¼ tsp strawberry extract
- The juice of half a lime
- 1 ½ cup cold water
- ½ cup ice

Directions

1. Put all of the ingredients into the serving glass and stir well.
2. Serve and enjoy.

Nutrition: Calories: 8 kcal; Fats: 0 g; Carbohydrates: 2 g; Protein: 0 g

17
Sensational Strawberry Medley

 5 minutes   0 minutes   2

Ingredients

- 1–2 handfuls baby greens
- 3 medium kale leaves
- 5–8 mint leaves
- 1-inch piece of ginger, peeled
- 1 avocado
- 1 cup strawberries
- 6–8 oz. coconut water + 6–8 oz. filtered water
- Fresh juice of 1 lime
- 1–2 tsp olive oil

Directions

1. Add all the ingredients to your blender.
2. Blend until smooth.
3. Add a few ice cubes and serve the smoothie.
4. **Enjoy!**

Nutrition: Calories: 255 kcal; Fats: 18 g; Carbohydrates: 22 g; Protein: 3 g

18
Simple Tofu Breakfast Scramble

10 minutes

20 minutes

2

Ingredients

FOR THE SCRAMBLE:
- 2 cups kale, roughly chopped
- 8 oz. extra-firm tofu
- ¼ red onion, thinly sliced
- ½ red pepper, thinly sliced
- 1–2 tbsp olive oil

FOR THE SAUCE:
- ½ tsp garlic powder
- ¼ tsp chili powder
- ½ tsp cumin powder
- ¼ tsp turmeric (optional)
- ½ tsp sea salt
- Water, for thinning

FOR THE SERVING (OPTIONAL):
- Salsa
- Cilantro
- Fruits (100 g)

Directions

1. Pat the tofu dry using a paper towel and roll in a clean kitchen towel. Put something heavy (e.g., cast-iron skillet) on top and leave for about 15 minutes.
2. Meanwhile, prepare the sauce by combining the spices and salt in a small bowl. Add enough water for a pourable consistency.
3. Heat oil in a large skillet placed over a medium heat. Sauté the onions and red pepper then season with salt. Continue to cook for about 5 minutes or until the veggies are tender.
4. Add the kale, a bit more salt, and pepper then cover with a lid. Continue to cook for another 2 minutes.
5. Place the tofu on a plate and crumble it into bite-sized pieces with a fork.
6. Uncover the skillet and move the veggies to one side of the pan with a spatula. Add the tofu and sauté for 2 minutes.
7. Add the sauce, pouring more of it over the tofu and just a bit over the veggies. Stir and cook for another 5–7 minutes or until the tofu is slightly browned.
8. Serve with salsa, cilantro, and/or fruits if desired. You can also store it in a freezer for up to a month.

Nutrition: Calories: 221 kcal; Fats: 15g Carbohydrates: 13 g; Protein: 11 g

19
Strawberry Mint Infused Water

5 minutes   **5 minutes**   **1**

Ingredients

- 4 strawberries, sliced
- 1 cucumber, sliced
- 5 fresh mint leaves
- 2 cups water

Directions

1. Put the cucumber, strawberries, and mint in a glass jar.
2. Pour water into the jar and stir well.
3. Cover the jar with a lid and place it in the refrigerator for 1 hour.
4. Serve and enjoy.

Nutrition: Calories: 52 kcal; Fats: 0 g; Carbohydrates: 11 g; Protein: 2 g

20
Sweet Potato Waffles

5 minutes   **10 minutes**   **2**

Ingredients

- ½ a cup of sweet potato
- 1 cup oats
- 2 eggs
- 1 cup of almond milk
- 1 tbsp honey
- Maple syrup (based on your preference)
- 2 bananas, sliced
- ¼ tsp baking powder
- 1 tbsp olive oil
- Cooking spray

Directions

1. Combine all the ingredients in a blender jar. Blend them until fully pureed.
2. Heat the waffle iron and spray it with cooking spray.
3. Pour ⅓ cup of batter into each waffle mold and cook for 3–4 minutes.
4. Once cooked, serve with maple syrup and fresh, chopped banana.

Nutrition: Calories: 343 kcal; Fats: 10 g; Carbohydrates: 54 g; Protein: 12 g

21
Baked Broccoli and Eggs

 10 min   15 min   4

Ingredients

- 4 oz. margarine, light
- 10 oz. frozen broccoli, thawed and chopped
- 4 oz. jarred pimento, chopped
- 6 tbsp flour
- 1 pinch of freshly ground black pepper
- ½ cup of mushrooms, sliced
- 6 large eggs
- ½ lb. cheddar cheese, low-fat
- 1 lb. cottage cheese, non-fat
- 1 tsp salt
- 1 pinch of paprika

Directions

1. Pre-heat the oven to 350°F.
2. Meanwhile, place the eggs, broccoli, and all other ingredients in a large bowl.
3. Stir to combine.
4. Use cooking spray to coat the sides and bottom of a casserole dish (2-quart).
5. Fill the dish with the broccoli-egg mixture, making sure to spread it evenly.
6. Bake in the oven for 1 ½ hours.
7. Serve immediately.

Nutrition: Calories: 554 kcal; Fats: 42 g; Carbohydrates: 18 g; Protein: 26 g

22
Banana and Almond Flax Glass

5 minutes   **0 minutes**   **2**

Ingredients

- 1 ripe frozen banana, diced
- ⅔ cup unsweetened almond milk
- ⅓ cup fat-free plain Greek yogurt
- 1 tbsp almond butter
- 1 tbsp flaxseed
- 1 tsp honey
- 2–3 drops almond extract

Directions

1. Add the listed ingredients to your blender and blend until smooth
2. Serve chilled!

Nutrition: Calories: 192 kcal; Fats: 7 g; Carbohydrates: 27 g; Protein: 6.5 g

23
Basil Tea

5 minutes   **10 minutes**   **1**

Ingredients

- 1 tbsp basil, dried
- 1 cup water
- 1 tsp honey

Directions

1. Add basil to boiling water and set aside for 10 minutes.
2. Strain and add honey.
3. Stir well and serve hot.

Nutrition: Calories: 20 kcal; Fats: 0 g; Carbohydrates: 5,0 g; Protein: 0 g

24
Blackberry and Apple Smoothie

 5 minutes   0 minutes   2

Ingredients

- 2 cups blackberries, frozen
- ½ cup apple cider
- 1 apple, cubed
- ⅔ cup non-fat lemon yogurt

Directions

1. Add the listed ingredients to your blender and blend until smooth.
2. Serve chilled!

Nutrition: Calories: 180 kcal; Fats: 0.5 g; Carbohydrates: 40 g; Protein: 9 g

25
Blueberry Multigrain Pancakes

Note: Consider this a special treat and do not consume more than 1 a week!!

 20 minutes   30 minutes   2

Ingredients

- 1 cup blueberries, rinsed and dried
- ½ tsp vanilla extract
- ½ cup whole wheat flour
- ½ cup all-purpose flour
- ¼ cup barley or rye flour
- 1 tbsp and 1 tsp baking powder
- 1 cup plain, low-fat yogurt
- 2–4 tbsp low-fat milk
- 3 tbsp butter + extra for buttering the skillet
- 2 large eggs
- ½ tsp lemon zest
- 1 tbsp erythritol

Directions

1. Melt butter in a skillet on medium heat.
2. Combine eggs, yogurt, and 2 tbsp milk in a bowl. Add melted butter, zest, and vanilla extract.
3. Combine all flours, sugar, and baking powder in a bowl.
4. Combine dry ingredients with the wet ingredients until no lumps are left.
5. Preheat a skillet and melt 1 tbsp butter on medium heat.
6. Pour ¼ cup of batter at a time and make sure to leave some space between each pancake.
7. Put a few berries on top of each pancake and press it with a spatula to spread the batter.
8. Cook pancakes for 3–4 minutes till they are dry around the edges, then flip them and cook for 3 minutes, until golden underneath.
9. Once cooked, transfer pancakes onto a plate and serve.

Nutrition: Calories: 532kcal; Fats: 12 g; Carbohydrates: 85 g; Protein: 19 g

26
Morning Glory Smoothie

10 minutes

0 minutes

2

Ingredients

- 1 cup non-fat milk
- ½ cup 100% apple juice
- 2 tbsp walnuts, chopped
- 2 tbsp coconut flakes, unsweetened
- 2 bananas, frozen
- 1 small carrot, peeled and chopped
- ½ tsp cinnamon, ground
- ½ tsp pure vanilla extract
- ½ tsp stevia, granulated
- 1–2 cups ice cubes

Directions

1. Place the milk, apple juice, walnuts, and coconut flakes in the pitcher of a blender. Let it sit for 5 minutes.
2. Add the frozen bananas, carrot, cinnamon, vanilla extract, stevia, and ice cubes to the pitcher. Purée until smooth.
3. Serve immediately.

Nutrition: Calories: 273 kcal; Fats: 6.5 g; Carbohydrates: 51 g; Protein: 8 g

27
Peach Avocado Smoothie

13 minutes

0 minutes

2

Ingredients

- 1 cup peaches, frozen
- 1 cup non-fat milk
- 1 cup vanilla Greek yogurt
- 1 avocado, peeled and pitted
- 1 tbsp flaxseed, ground
- 1 tsp stevia, granulated
- 1 tsp pure vanilla extract
- 1–2 cups ice cubes

Directions

1. Combine all the ingredients in a blender. Purée until smooth.
2. Serve immediately.

Nutrition: Calories: 281 kcal; Fats: 12 g; Carbohydrates: 28 g; Protein: 16 g

28
Strawberry and Clementine Glass

 5 minutes   0 minutes   2

Ingredients

- 8 oz. strawberries, fresh
- 1 banana, chopped into chunks
- 2 clementines/mandarins

Directions

1. Peel the clementines and remove the seeds.
2. Put the listed ingredients in your blender/food processor and blend until smooth.
3. Serve chilled and enjoy!

Nutrition: Calories: 134 kcal; Fats: 1 g; Carbohydrates: 33g; Protein: 2 g

29
The Mean Green Smoothie

 5 minutes   0 minutes   2

Ingredients

- 1 avocado
- 1 handful spinach, chopped
- 1 cucumber, peeled and cut into 2-inch slices
- 1 lime, chopped
- A handful of grapes, chopped
- 5 dates, stoned and chopped
- 1 cup fresh apple juice

Directions

1. Add all the ingredients to your blender.
2. Blend until smooth.
3. Add a few ice cubes and serve the smoothie.
4. **Enjoy!**

Nutrition: Calories: 364 kcal; Fats: 11 g; Carbohydrates: 70 g; Protein: 4 g

30
The Minty Refresher

 5 minutes   0 minutes   2

Ingredients

- 2 cups mint tea
- 1 cucumber, peeled
- 2 green apples
- 1 cup blueberries
- Stevia (to sweeten)
- A few slices of lime/lemon for garnish

Directions

1. Put the listed ingredients in your blender and blend until smooth.
2. Add ice and sweeten with a bit of stevia.
3. Garnish with lime/lemon slices.
4. Serve and enjoy!

Nutrition: Calories: 161 kcal; Fats: 0.5 g; Carbohydrates: 38 g; Protein: 2 g

31
Watermelon Mint Infused Water

 5 minutes   5 minutes   4

Ingredients

- 1 cup watermelon, sliced
- 4 cups water
- 8 fresh mint leaves

Directions

1. Put the mint and watermelon in a glass jar.
2. Pour water into the jar and cover with a lid.
3. Place the jar in the refrigerator for 1 hour.
4. Serve and enjoy.

Nutrition: Calories: 12 kcal; Fats: 0 g; Carbohydrates: 3.1 g; Protein: 0 g

32
Rice Puddi

10 minutes

25 minutes

2

Ingredients

- 6 cups water
- 1 cup coconut sugar
- 2 cups black rice
- 2 pears, cored and cubed
- 2 tsp cinnamon powder

Directions

1. Put the water in a pan and heat it over medium-high heat.
2. Add the rice, sugar, and the other ingredients.
3. Stir, bring to a simmer, reduce the heat to medium and cook for 25 minutes.
4. Divide into bowls and serve cold.

Note: Consider it a special treat and do not consume it more than 1 a week

Nutrition: Calories: 689 kcal; Fats: 2 g; Carbohydrates: 192 g; Protein: 7 g

Chapter 2
LUNCH

33
Cheesy Black Bean Wraps

 5 minutes   15 minutes   2

Ingredients

- 2 tbsp green chili peppers, chopped
- 4 green onions, diced
- 1 tomato, diced
- 1 tbsp garlic, chopped
- 6 tortilla wraps, whole grain, and fat-free
- ¾ cup cheddar cheese, shredded
- ¾ cup salsa
- ½ cup corn kernels
- 3 tbsp cilantro, fresh and chopped
- ½ cup black beans, canned and drained

Directions

1. Toss your chili peppers, corn, black beans, garlic, tomato, onions, and cilantro in a bowl.
2. Heat the mixture in a microwave for a minute, and stir for ½ minute.
3. Spread the 2 tortillas between paper towels and microwave for 20 seconds.
4. Warm the remaining tortillas the same way, and add ½ cup of bean mixture, 2 tbsp of salsa, and 2 tbsp of cheese for each tortilla. Roll them up before serving.

Nutrition: Calories: 1150kcal; Carbohydrates: 21,5 g; Protein: 19 g; Fats: 34 g

34
Cilantro Lime Shrimp

10 minutes   **15 minutes**   **2**

Ingredients

- 1 lb. shrimp, peeled and deveined
- 2 tsp lime zest
- ⅓ cup lime juice
- ⅓ cup fresh cilantro, chopped
- 1 jalapeno pepper, seeded and minced
- 2 tbsp olive oil
- 3 garlic cloves, minced
- ¼ tsp ground cumin
- ¼ tsp ground black pepper
- Lime slices, for serving

Directions

1. Mix lime zest and juice, cilantro, jalapeno, oil, garlic, cumin, and pepper in a bowl. Add shrimp and toss well to combine.
2. Refrigerate for 15 minutes.
3. Preheat the grill to medium-high heat and thread the shrimp onto skewers.
4. Grill for about 3–4 minutes per side and serve topped with more cilantro.
5. Serve with lime slices.

Nutrition: Calories: 355 kcal; Fats: 13 g; Carbohydrates: 26 g; Protein: 55 g

35
Egg Casserole with Onions, Mushrooms, and Broccoli

| 10 minutes | 40 minutes | 6 |

Ingredients

- 1 cup onions, chopped
- 12 oz. mushrooms, cooked
- 12 eggs
- 1 cup broccoli, diced
- ¼ cup low-fat milk
- 1 cup cheese, shredded
- ½ tsp dried oregano
- ½ tsp dried thyme
- ½ tsp basil, dried
- 1 cup chicken, shredded

Directions

1. Preheat the oven to 375°F.
2. Put the onions in a pan and fry until translucent.
3. Add the broccoli and mushrooms and cook for a few minutes.
4. In a large bowl mix the herbs, milk, and eggs.
5. Add the shredded cheese, chicken, and cooked vegetables to the bowl.
6. Now add this mixture into a nonstick pan and bake for 30-35 minutes.
7. Your dish is ready to be served.

Nutrition: Calories: 296 kcal; Fats: 15 g; Carbohydrates: 7,6 g; Protein: 21 g

36
Bacon Jalapeño Poppers

| 10 minutes | 8 minutes | 4 |

Ingredients

- 4 lean bacon strips, cut in half
- 4 jalapeño peppers, cut in half with seeds removed
- ⅓ cup of softened light cream cheese.
- 1 tbsp fresh rosemary, finely chopped
- Cooking spray

Directions

1. Preheat the air fryer to 370°F.
2. In a small bowl, stir the cream cheese and rosemary until well mixed.
3. Stuff cream cheese into each jalapeño half.
4. Wrap each jalapeño half with a bacon strip and place in the oil-sprayed air fryer basket.
5. Cook for 6–8 minutes.
6. Serve and enjoy.

Nutrition: Calories: 87 kcal; Fats: 6.5 g; Carbohydrates: 2,25 g; Protein: 5 g

37
Barley and Lentil Stew

 15 minutes   50 minutes   4

Ingredients

- 2 tbsp olive oil
- 2 carrots, peeled and chopped
- 1 large onion, chopped
- 2 celery stalks, chopped
- 2 garlic cloves, minced
- 1 tsp ground coriander
- 2 tsp ground cumin
- 1 tsp cayenne pepper
- 1 cup barley
- 1 cup red lentils
- 1 (14-oz.) can tomatoes, diced with liquid
- 8 cups low-fat vegetable broth
- 4 cups of fresh spinach, torn
- Salt and ground black pepper, as needed

Directions

1. In a heavy-bottomed saucepan, warm oil over medium heat and sauté carrots, onion, and celery for about 5 minutes.
2. Add garlic and spices and sauté for about 1 minute.
3. Add barley, lentils, tomatoes, and broth, and bring to a boil.
4. Now adjust the heat to low and simmer, covered, for about 40 minutes.
5. Stir in spinach, salt, and black pepper, and simmer for about 3–4 minutes.
6. Serve hot.

Nutrition: Calories: 226 kcal; Fats: 7.75 g; Saturated Fats: 1.1 g; Carbohydrates: 33 g; Protein: 9 g

38
Beef Steak Nuggets

30 minutes to chill

18 minutes

4

Ingredients

- 1 lb. beef steak, cut into chunks
- 1 large egg
- ½ cup parmesan cheese, grated
- 2 cups low-carb breadcrumbs
- 1 tbsp rosemary, dried
- 1 tbsp dried thyme
- A pinch sea salt
- A pinch black pepper
- Cooking spray

Directions

1. Whisk the egg and black pepper in a small bowl.
2. In a shallow bowl, mix together breadcrumbs, cheese, rosemary, thyme, and salt.
3. Dip each steak chunk in egg then coat with the breadcrumbs mixture and place on a plate. Let it sit in the refrigerator for 30 minutes.
4. Preheat the air fryer to 400°F. Spray the basket with cooking spray.
5. Place steak nuggets in the air fryer basket and cook for 15–18 minutes or until golden, shaking every 4 minutes.

Nutrition: Calories: 337 kcal; Fats: 9 g; Carbohydrates: 27 g; Protein: 35 g

39
Blackberry Crisp

20 minutes

5 minutes

2

Ingredients

- 1 cup crunchy granola
- 2 cups blackberries
- ⅓ cup powdered erythritol
- 2 tbsp lemon juice
- ¼ tsp xanthan gum

Directions

1. Take a large bowl, and toss blackberries, erythritol, lemon juice, and xanthan gum.
2. Pour into a 6-inch round baking dish and cover with foil. Place in the air fryer basket.
3. Adjust the temperature to 350°F and set the timer for 12 minutes. When the timer beeps, remove the foil and stir.
4. Sprinkle granola over the mixture and return to the air fryer basket. Adjust the temperature to 320°F and set the timer for 3 minutes or until the top is golden. Serve warm.

Nutrition: Calories: 356 kcal; Fats: 14 g; Carbohydrates: 77 g; Protein: 14 g

40
Broiled White Fish Parmesan

10 minutes   **15 minutes**   **4**

Ingredients

- 3 oz. codfish
- ¼ cup parmesan cheese, grated
- 2 tbsp light margarine, softened
- ⅛ tsp garlic salt
- ⅛ tsp ground black pepper
- 1 tbsp lemon juice
- 1 tbsp mayonnaise
- ⅛ tsp dried basil
- ⅛ tsp, onion powder
- Cooking spray

Directions

1. Set the grill at a high temperature and preheat before starting cooking.
2. Grease the broiling pot with cooking spray.
3. Combine butter, parmesan cheese, lemon juice, and mayonnaise.
4. Season with pepper, onion powder, dried basil, and garlic salt.
5. Mix it well and keep it ready to use.
6. Layer the fillets on the broiler pan and broil for 2–3 minutes.
7. Set it and cook for another 2–3 minutes.
8. Remove the baked fillets from the grill onto a plate and transfer the parmesan mixture over it.
9. Again, broil it for a couple of minutes until the topping becomes brown.
10. Serve hot, when the flakes can be easily removed.

Nutrition: Calories: 77 kcal; Carbohydrates: 1 g; Protein: 6 g; Fats: 5.5g

41
Catfish with Cajun Seasoning

5 minutes   **20 minutes**   **4**

Ingredients

- 3 tsp Cajun seasoning
- ¾ cup Cornmeal
- 4 catfish fillets

Directions

1. Pre-heat the oven at 390°F
2. Put Cajun seasoning and cornmeal in a zip lock bag.
3. Wash and pat the catfish fillets dry. Add them to the zip lock bag.
4. Coat the fillets well with the seasoning. Put the fillets in the air fryer.
5. Cook the fillets within 15 minutes and turn them halfway through.
6. To get a golden color on the fillets, cook for 5 more minutes.
7. Serve with lemon wedges and spicy tartar sauce.

Nutrition: Calories: 189 kcal; Fats: 2,25 g; Carbohydrates: 25 g; Protein: 18 g

42
Chickpea and Pumpkin Curry

 15 minutes   35 minutes   4

Ingredients

- 1 tbsp olive oil
- 1 onion, chopped
- 2 garlic cloves, minced
- 1 green chili, seeded and finely chopped
- 1 tsp ground cumin
- ½ tsp ground coriander
- 1 tsp red chili powder
- 2 cups fresh tomatoes, finely chopped
- 2 lb. pumpkin, peeled and cubed
- 2 cups vegetable broth
- 2 cups canned chickpeas, rinsed and drained
- Ground salt and black pepper
- 2 tbsp fresh lemon juice
- 2 tbsp fresh cilantro leaves, chopped

Directions

1. In a heavy-bottomed saucepan, warm the oil over medium-high heat and sauté onion for about 5–7 minutes.
2. Add garlic, green chili, spices, and sauté for about 1 minute.
3. Add tomatoes and cook for 2–3 minutes, crushing with the back of a spoon.
4. Add the pumpkin and cook for about 3–4 minutes, stirring occasionally.
5. Add broth and bring to a boil.
6. Now adjust the heat to low and simmer for about 10 minutes.
7. Stir in the chickpeas and simmer for about 10 minutes.
8. Stir in the salt, black pepper, and lemon juice, and serve hot with a garnish of cilantro.

Nutrition: Calories: 210 kcal; Fats: 11 g; Saturated Fats: 1.3 g; Carbohydrates: 23.5 g; Protein: 12 g

43
Chickpeas Salad

 15 minutes   15 minutes   4

Ingredients

SALAD:
- 1 can chickpeas, drained and rinsed
- 1 head butter lettuce, shredded
- 1 large cucumber, chopped
- 1 red bell pepper, seeded and chopped
- 1 cup of tomatoes, chopped
- 1 red onion, chopped
- 2 tbsp fresh cilantro leaves, chopped
- 2 tbsp fresh mint leaves, chopped

DRESSING:
- 1 Serrano pepper, seeded and minced
- 1 garlic clove, minced
- ¼ cup extra-virgin olive oil
- 3 tbsp red wine vinegar
- 1 tbsp fresh lemon juice
- ¼ tsp red pepper flakes, crushed
- Ground salt and black pepper, as needed

Directions

1. The salad: in a salad bowl, add all ingredients and mix.
2. The dressing: in another bowl, add all ingredients and beat until well combined.
3. Pour the dressing over the salad and toss gently to coat well.
4. Serve immediately.

Nutrition: Calories: 164 kcal; Fats: 7,5 g; Carbohydrates: 20 g; Protein: 12 g

44
Chipotle Shredded Pork

 10 minutes   6 hours   4

Ingredients

- 2 lb. pork shoulder, trimmed of excess fat
- 1 (7.5 oz.) can of chipotle peppers in adobo sauce
- 1 tbsp apple cider vinegar
- 1 tbsp ground cumin
- 1 tbsp dried oregano
- ½ tbsp juniper berries
- 1 lime, juiced

Directions

1. In a blender, purée the chipotle peppers in adobo sauce, apple cider vinegar, cumin, oregano, juniper, and lime juice.
2. Place the pork shoulder in the slow cooker and pour the sauce over the top.
3. Place a lid on the slow cooker and cook on LOW for 6 hours.
4. With the help of 2 forks, shred the pork in the slow cooker.
5. If there is any sauce left, cook the pork on LOW for 20 minutes.

Nutrition: Calories: 445 kcal; Fats: 25 g; Carbohydrates: 6.5 g; Protein: 41 g

45
Cooked Ham Mousse

 5 minutes   0 minutes   1

Ingredients

- 4 oz. extra-lean cooked ham slices
- 2 tbsp low-fat ricotta cheese
- 1 tsp fresh finely chopped parsley
- ½ tsp low-salt capers
- ½ tbsp lime juice
- A pinch of white pepper

Directions

1. Place the cooked ham slices and ricotta in a mixer and pulse until soft.
2. Add all the other ingredients and continue mixing until a puréed consistency is reached.

Nutrition: Calories: 126 kcal; Fats: 5 g; Carbohydrates: 3 g; Protein: 21 g

46
Creamy Beef Stroganoff with Mushrooms

10 minutes   **30 minutes**   **3**

Ingredients

- Nonstick cooking spray
- 1 lb. extra-lean beef sirloin, cut into ½-inch strips
- 1 tsp extra-virgin olive oil
- 1 medium onion, chopped
- ½ lb. mushrooms, sliced
- 2 tbsp whole-wheat flour
- 1 cup low-sodium beef broth
- 1 cup water
- 1 tsp Worcestershire sauce
- ½ tsp dried thyme
- ½ tsp dried dill
- ½ cup low-fat plain Greek yogurt
- 2 tbsp fresh parsley, finely chopped, for garnish

Directions

1. Coat a medium pan with the cooking spray and place over a medium-high heat.
2. Add the beef and cook, stirring frequently, until browned, about 5 minutes.
3. Transfer to a bowl and set aside.
4. In the same pan, heat the olive oil over medium-high heat. Add the onion and cook until tender, 1 to 2 minutes.
5. Add the mushrooms and cook until tender, about 3 minutes.
6. Mix in the flour and stir to coat the onion and mushrooms.
7. Stir in the broth, water, Worcestershire sauce, thyme, and dill. Bring to a boil, cover the pan, and cook for about 10 minutes, stirring frequently.
8. Stir in the yogurt. Mix in the beef.
9. Serve, garnished with the parsley.

Nutrition: Calories: 443 kcal; Fats: 25 g; Carbohydrates: 13 g; Protein: 41 g

47
Creamy Beef with Mushrooms

 10 minutes   25 minutes   3

Ingredients

- 1 ½ lb extra-lean beef sirloin, cut into ½-inch strips
- 1 medium onion, chopped
- ½ lb. mushrooms, sliced
- 2 tbsp whole-wheat flour
- 1 cup low-sodium beef broth
- 1 cup water
- 1 tsp low-sodium Worcestershire sauce
- ½ tsp dried thyme
- ½ tsp dried dill
- ½ cup low-fat plain Greek yogurt
- 1 tsp Dijon mustard
- ¼ tsp ground red pepper
- Cooking spray
- 2 tbsp fresh parsley, finely chopped (for garnish)

Directions

1. Spray a medium pan with the cooking oil and place over medium-high heat.
2. Add the beef and cook, stirring frequently, for about 5 minutes until browned. Transfer to a bowl and set aside.
3. In the same pan, spray oil, if needed, and heat over medium-high.
4. Add the onion and cook until tender, about 2–3 minutes.
5. Add the mushrooms and cook until tender, for about 3 minutes.
6. Mix in the flour and stir to coat the onion and mushrooms.
7. Pour in broth, water, Worcestershire sauce, thyme, ground red pepper, and dill, and stir well.
8. Bring to a boil, cover the pan, lower the heat and cook for about 10 minutes, stirring frequently.
9. In a small bowl, mix yogurt and mustard.
10. Stir the yogurt and mustard mixture in the pan.
11. Mix in the beef and serve, garnished with the parsley.

Nutrition: Calories: 357 kcal; Fats: 16 g; Carbohydrates: 30 g; Protein: 27 g

48
Crispy Fish Sandwich

15 minutes   **10 minutes**   **2**

Ingredients

- 2 fillets of cod
- 2 tbsp all-purpose flour
- ¼ tsp pepper
- 1 tbsp lemon juice
- ¼ tsp salt
- ½ tsp garlic powder
- 1 egg
- ½ tbsp mayo
- ½ cup whole wheat breadcrumbs

Directions

1. Preheat the oven at 400°F
2. In a bowl, add salt, flour, pepper, and garlic powder. In a separate bowl, add lemon juice, mayo, and egg. In another bowl, add the breadcrumbs.
3. Coat the fish in flour, then in egg, then in breadcrumbs. With cooking oil, spray the basket and put the fish in the basket.
4. Also, spray the fish with cooking oil. Cook for 10 minutes. This fish is soft so be careful if you choose to flip it.

Nutrition: Calories: 276 kcal; Fats: 5.5 g Carbohydrates: 20.5 g; Protein: 32 g

49
Fajita Pork Strips

10 minutes   **35 minutes**   **2**

Ingredients

- 16 oz. pork sirloin
- 1 tbsp fajita seasonings
- 1 tbsp canola oil

Directions

1. Preheat the oven at 365°F
2. Cut the pork sirloin into strips and sprinkle with fajita seasonings and canola oil.
3. Then transfer the meat to the baking tray in one layer.
4. Bake it for 35 minutes. Stir the meat every 10 minutes during cooking.

Nutrition: Calories: 282 kcal; Fats: 6 g; Carbohydrates: 1.5 g; Protein: 50 g

50
Fresh Tomato and Celery Soup

 10 minutes   30 minutes   4

Ingredients

- 1 lb. tomatoes, peeled and roughly chopped
- 1 oz. celery root, finely chopped
- ¼ cup fresh celery leaves, finely chopped
- 1 tbsp fresh basil, finely chopped
- Salt and pepper, to taste
- 5 tbsp extra virgin olive oil

Directions

1. Preheat the oil in a large non-stick frying pan over a medium-high temperature. Add finely chopped celery root, celery leaves, and fresh basil.
2. Season with salt and pepper and stir-fry for about 10 minutes, until nicely browned.
3. Add chopped tomatoes and about ¼ cup of water. Reduce the heat to a minimum and cook for 15 minutes, stirring constantly, until softened.
4. Now add about 4 cups of water (or vegetable broth) and bring it to a boil. Give it a good stir and remove it from the heat.
5. Top with fresh parsley and serve.

Nutrition: Calories: 174 kcal; Fats: 17 g; Carbohydrates: 5,25g; Protein: 1,25 g

51
Garlic Pork Meatballs

 10 minutes   28 minutes   2

Ingredients

- 2 pork medallions
- 1 tsp cayenne pepper
- 1 tbsp olive oil
- ¼ cup coconut milk
- 1 tsp garlic, minced

Directions

1. Sprinkle each pork medallion with cayenne pepper.
2. Heat up olive oil in the skillet and add meat.
3. Roast the pork medallions for 3 minutes from each side.
4. After this, add coconut milk and minced garlic. Close the lid and simmer the meat for 20 minutes on low heat.

Nutrition: Calories: 198 kcal; Fats: 13 g; Carbohydrates: 1 g; Protein: 20 g

52
Roast and Mushrooms

5 minutes   **25 minutes**   **2**

Ingredients

- ½ lb. pork roast
- 13 oz. mushrooms, sliced
- 12 oz. low-sodium beef stock
- 1 tsp Italian seasoning

Directions

1. Preheat the oven at 350°F
2. In a roasting pan, combine the roast with mushrooms, stock, and Italian seasoning, and toss.
3. Put in the oven and bake for 1 hour 20 minutes.
4. Slice the roast, dividing the mushroom mix between plates and serve.
5. Enjoy!

Nutrition: Calories: 318 kcal; Fats: 16 g; Carbohydrates: 3 g; Protein: 36 g

53
Greek Beef Roast

10 minutes   **8 hours**   **6**

Ingredients

- 2 lb. lean top round beef
- 1 tbsp Italian seasoning
- 6 garlic cloves, minced
- 1 onion, sliced
- 2 cups beef broth
- ½ cup red wine
- 1 tsp red pepper flakes
- Pepper, to taste
- Salt, to taste

Directions

1. Season meat with pepper and salt and place in the pot.
2. Pour the remaining ingredients over the meat.
3. Cook on low for 8 hours. Shred the meat using a fork. Serve and enjoy.

Nutrition: Calories: 295 kcal; Fats: 18 g; Carbohydrates: 5 g; Protein: 29 g

54
Greek Pork Chops

10 minutes

6 minutes

4

Ingredients

- 8 pork chops, boneless
- 4 tsp dried oregano
- 2 tbsp Worcestershire sauce
- 3 tbsp fresh lemon juice
- ¼ cup olive oil
- 1 tsp ground mustard
- 2 tsp garlic powder
- 2 tsp onion powder
- Pepper, to taste
- Salt, to taste

Directions

1. Whisk together oil, garlic powder, onion powder, oregano, Worcestershire sauce, lemon juice, mustard, pepper, and salt.
2. Place pork chops in a dish, then pour the marinade over the pork chops and coat well. Place in the refrigerator overnight—Preheat the grill.
3. Put pork chops on the grill and cook for 3–4 minutes on each side. Serve and enjoy.

Nutrition: Calories: 257 kcal; Fats: 14 g; Carbohydrates: 3 g; Protein: 26 g

55
Green Beans

5 minutes

13 minutes

2

Ingredients

- 1 lb. green beans
- ¾ tsp garlic powder
- ¾ tsp ground black pepper
- 1 tsp salt
- ½ tsp paprika
- Olive oil, to taste

Directions

1. Turn on an air fryer, insert the basket, grease with olive oil, close the lid and set it at 400°F. Preheat for 5 minutes.
2. Meanwhile, put the beans in a bowl, sprinkle generously with olive oil, sprinkle with garlic powder, black pepper, salt, and paprika, and stir until well coated.
3. Open the air fryer, add the green beans, close with the lid and cook for 8 minutes until golden and crisp, stirring halfway through the frying process.
4. When the fryer beeps, open the lid, transfer the green beans to a serving plate and serve.

Nutrition: Calories: 137 kcal; Fats: 7 g Carbohydrates: 17 g; Protein: 4 g

56
Green Buddha Bowl

 15 minutes
 0 minutes
 2

Ingredients

- 1 tbsp olive oil
- 1 lb. Brussels sprouts, trimmed and halved
- Salt and black pepper, to taste
- 2 cups cooked quinoa
- 1 cup red apple, chopped
- ¼ cup pepitas
- 1 avocado, sliced
- 1 ½ cup arugula
- ½ cup mayo
- ¾ cup plain Greek yogurt
- 1 tsp ground mustard
- ¼ cup Pompeian white balsamic vinegar
- ½ tsp salt
- 1 tbsp chopped fresh basil
- 1 garlic clove, minced

Directions

1. Mix the quinoa with apple and the rest of the ingredients in a salad bowl.
2. Serve.
3. **Serving suggestion:** Serve the bowl with spaghetti squash.
4. **Variation tip:** Add some edamame beans to the bowl.

Nutrition: Calories: 357 kcal; Fats: 19 g; Carbohydrates: 35 g; Protein: 8 g

57
Green Cream Soup

5 minutes

15 minutes

2

Ingredients

- 1 cup fresh broccoli, chopped
- 1 cup cauliflower, chopped
- 4 tbsp fresh parsley, finely chopped
- ¼ tsp chili pepper, ground
- 1 tsp dried thyme
- ½ cup milk, low-fat

Directions

1. Place broccoli and cauliflower in a heavy-bottomed pot. Add enough water to cover all the ingredients and bring to a boil. Cook for 5 minutes, or until tender. Remove from the heat and drain well. Set aside to cool for a while.
2. Transfer cooked broccoli and cauliflower to a blender. Add ½ cup of water and sprinkle with chili pepper. Process until pureed and transfer to a clean, heavy-bottomed pot.
3. Add 2 cups of water and sprinkle with finely chopped parsley. Bring to a boil and reduce the heat to low. Cook for 2 minutes. Add milk and give it a good stir. Cook for 5 more minutes over medium-high heat.
4. Serve warm.

Nutrition: Calories: 63 kcal; Fats: 1 g; Carbohydrates: 9.5 g; Protein: 4.6 g

58
Grilled Chicken Wings

15 minutes

20 minutes

8

Ingredients

- ½ tsp garlic, minced
- 1 cup buffalo wing sauce
- 3 tbsp extra virgin olive oil
- 2 lb. chicken wings, frozen
- Freshly ground pepper, to taste.
- Salt to taste

Directions

1. Mix all the ingredients and leave them to stand, covered, for 10 minutes.
2. Now pour the olive oil on a grill and place the marinated wings on top.
3. Grill on both sides until crispy and brown.
4. Your dish is ready to be served.

Nutrition: Calories: 687 kcal; Fats: 43 g; Carbohydrates: 62 g; Protein: 9 g

59
Grilled Eggplants

 10 minutes   10 minutes   2

Ingredients

- 1 large eggplant, cut into thick circles
- Salt and pepper to taste
- 1 tsp smoked paprika
- 1 tbsp coconut flour
- 1 tsp lime juice
- 1 tbsp olive oil

Directions

1. Coat the eggplants in smoked paprika, salt, pepper, lime juice, and coconut flour and let them sit for 10 minutes.
2. Pour the olive oil into a grilling pan.
3. Grill the eggplants for 3 minutes on each side.
4. Serve.

Nutrition: Fats: 8 g; Carbohydrates: 16 g; Protein: 3 g

60
Herb Pork Roast

 10 minutes   14 hours   5

Ingredients

- 5 lb. pork roast, boneless or bone-in
- 1 tbsp Italian dry herb mix
- 4 garlic cloves, cut into slivers
- 1 tbsp salt

Directions

1. Using a knife, make small slices all over the meat, then insert garlic slivers into the cuts. In a small bowl, mix Italian herb mix and salt and rub all over the pork roast.
2. Place the pork roast in the pot. Cook on low for 14 hours. Extract meat from the pot and shred using a fork. Serve and enjoy.

Nutrition: Calories: 610 kcal; Fats: 24 g; Carbohydrates: 1.6 g; Protein: 93 g

61
Herb-Roasted Pork Loin and Potatoes

5 minutes   **1 hour**   **2**

Ingredients

- 1 (1 lb./454 g) pork loin, trimmed
- 8 garlic cloves
- ¼ cup olive oil, divided
- Black pepper, freshly ground, to taste
- 1 cup cubed raw sweet potato
- 1 cup small gold potatoes, quartered
- 8 fresh thyme sprigs, chopped
- Nonstick cooking spray

Directions

1. Preheat the oven to 350°F. Rub the pork with garlic and 2 tbsp olive oil. Season with black pepper. Coat a 9-x-13-inch baking dish with nonstick cooking spray.
2. Place the pork in the prepared baking dish. Bake for approximately 60 minutes, or until an instant-read thermometer inserted in the center registers 145°F.
3. 20 minutes into the cooking time, place the cubed and sliced sweet potatoes and gold potatoes on a rimmed baking dish, drizzle with the remaining olive oil, sprinkle with the thyme, and place in the oven. The potatoes should have finished roasting at about the same time as the pork and should be tender and slightly browned.
4. Once the pork is finished cooking, remove it from the oven and let the meat stand for 15 minutes before carving. Cut into 8 slices. Serve with roasted potatoes and a green salad.

Nutrition: Calories: 612 kcal; Fats: 38 g; Carbohydrates: 27 g; Protein: 49 g

62
Homemade Chicken Soup

20 minutes | 40 minutes | 4

Ingredients

- 1 lb. chicken meat
- ½ cup soup noodles
- 4 cups chicken broth
- A handful of fresh parsley
- 1 tsp salt
- ¼ tsp black pepper, freshly ground

Directions

1. For this recipe, try to find an organic chicken. They are much tastier and better for a homemade soup. Use both dark and white pieces and rinse well under the running water. Pat dry with kitchen paper and place on a clean work surface.
2. Using a sharp paring knife, cut the chicken into bite-sized pieces. Sprinkle with salt and place in a deep pot. If using organic chicken, be careful not to add extra fat because this meat already has enough fat.
3. Pour in the chicken broth and cover with a lid. Cook for 45 minutes, over medium-high heat.
4. Now add soup noodles and reduce the heat to the minimum. Cook for 5 more minutes.
5. Sprinkle with some freshly ground black pepper and parsley.
6. Serve warm.

Nutrition: Calories: 182 kcal; Fats: 6 g; Carbohydrates: 8.75 g; Protein: 25 g

63
Lean Mean Soup

15 minutes

30 minutes

2

Ingredients

- ½ head cabbage, chopped
- 3 cups broccoli, chopped
- 1 cup carrots, diced
- 8 stalks celery, diced
- 1 cup onion, diced
- 1 cup radishes, chopped
- ½ cup yellow pepper, diced
- ½ cup red pepper, diced
- ½ cup orange pepper, diced
- 2 tbsp garlic, minced
- 1 (6 oz.) can tomato paste
- 2 (4 oz.) cans of chopped tomatoes with green chiles, undrained
- 6 ½ cups of water
- 1 tsp dried parsley
- 1 tsp dried oregano
- 1 tsp turmeric
- ½ cup kale
- Salt and black pepper, to taste

Directions

1. Add all the green soup ingredients to a cooking pot.
2. Cook for 30 minutes on low heat until the veggies are soft.
3. Serve warm.
4. **Serving suggestion:** Serve the soup with cauliflower rice.
5. **Variation tip:** Add broccoli florets to the soup as well.

Nutrition: Calories: 221 kcal; Fats: 1,5 g; Carbohydrates: 48 g; Protein: 12 g

64
Lemon Chicken

10 minutes **15 minutes** **2**

Ingredients

- 4 chicken breast fillets
- 1 large lemon
- 2 tsp fresh thyme leaves
- 1 ½ tbsp honey
- 2 tbsp water
- Salt and pepper, to taste

Directions

1. Preheat your grill to a high temperature and grease a shallow baking dish.
2. Place the chicken in the dish with the skin side face down.
3. Season chicken with salt and black pepper and grill for 5 minutes.
4. Meanwhile, thinly slice the lemon.
5. Turn the chicken pieces and place the lemon slice on top of each.
6. Season the chicken with honey, lemon juice, 2 tbsp water, seasoning, and thyme.
7. Return the baking dish to the grill and grill the chicken for 10 minutes.
8. Serve warm.

Nutrition: Calories: 520kcal; Fats: 26 g; Carbohydrates: 6 g; Protein: 60 g

65
Lemon Pepper Pork Tenderloin

10 minutes **25 minutes** **3**

Ingredients

- 1 lb. pork tenderloin
- ¾ tsp lemon pepper
- 2 tsp dried oregano
- 1 tbsp olive oil
- 3 tbsp feta cheese, crumbled
- 3 tbsp olive tapenade

Directions

1. Put pork, oil, lemon pepper, and oregano in a Ziploc bag and rub well. Then, place in a refrigerator for 2 hours.
2. Remove pork from the Ziploc bag. Make a lengthwise slice through the center of the tenderloin using a sharp knife. Spread olive tapenade on half of the tenderloin and sprinkle with feta cheese.
3. Fold another half of the meat over the original shape of the tenderloin. Tie the pork tenderloin with twine at 2-inch intervals.
4. Grill the pork tenderloin for 20 minutes. Cut into slices and serve.

Nutrition: Calories: 391 kcal; Fats: 9 g; Carbohydrates: 2.3 g; Protein: 32 g

66
Moroccan Chicken

 10 minutes   25 minutes   4

Ingredients

- 2 lb. chicken breasts, cut into chunks
- ½ tsp cinnamon
- 1 tsp turmeric
- ½ tsp ginger
- 1 tsp cumin
- 2 tbsp Dijon mustard
- 1 tbsp molasses
- 1 tbsp honey
- 2 tbsp tomato paste
- 5 garlic cloves, finely chopped
- 2 onions, cut into quarters
- 2 green bell peppers, cut into strips
- 2 red bell peppers, cut into strips
- 2 cups olives, pitted
- 1 lemon, peeled and sliced
- 2 tbsp olive oil
- Pepper to taste
- Salt to taste

Directions

1. Put the oil into the inner pot of the Instant Pot and set the pot on "Sauté" mode.
2. Add chicken and sauté for 5 minutes.
3. Add the remaining ingredients and stir everything well.
4. Seal the pot with a lid and select "Manual" and set the timer for 20 minutes. Once done, release the pressure using quick release. Remove the lid. Stir well and serve.

Nutrition: Calories: 396 kcal; Fats: 12 g; Carbohydrates: 17 g; Protein: 52 g

67
Pineapple Pork

10 minutes   **6 hours**   **4**

Ingredients

- 32 oz. lean pork shoulder, cut into chunks
- 1 onion, halved and sliced
- 1 cup pineapple, crushed
- 2 tbsp maple syrup
- 2 garlic cloves, crushed
- 2 tsp fresh ginger, grated
- ¼ cup soy sauce
- 2 tbsp tomato paste
- 1 tbsp sambal oelek (chili paste)
- ½ cup water
- 1 red pepper, sliced
- 1 green pepper, sliced
- 1 tbsp cornstarch
- Black pepper and salt to taste

Directions

1. in a bowl mix the crushed pineapple with the maple syrup, tomato paste, soy sauce, sambal oelek, ginger and garlic.
2. Add the onion and pork into a Slow Cooker then pour the pineapple mixture on top.
3. Mix evenly, then cover and cook on high for 5 hours.
4. Mix the cornstarch with water and add to the pork along with peppers.
5. Stir well, cover again, and cook on high for 1 hour.
6. Adjust the seasoning with black pepper and salt, then serve warm.

Nutrition: Calories: 423 kcal; Fats: 17 g; Carbohydrates: 18 g; Protein: 47 g

68
Pork Medallions

 10 minutes

 18 minutes

 3

Ingredients

- 1 cup sun-dried tomato and oregano dressing
- 1 cup frozen sliced green beans
- 1 (10 oz.) can chicken broth
- 1 cup instant white rice, uncooked
- 1 (1 lb.) pork tenderloin, cut crosswise into 8 slices
- 1 tsp dried rosemary leaves, crushed
- 1 cup chopped plum tomatoes
- 2 tbsp parmesan cheese, grated

Directions

1. Add 2 tbsp dressing and beans to a saucepan and cook for 1 minute on medium heat.
2. Stir in the broth and cook to a boil.
3. Reduce the heat to medium-low then let it simmer for 3 minutes.
4. Stir in the rice, boil again and then reduce the heat.
5. Cover and leave for 5 minutes and set the rice aside.
6. Season the meat slices with rosemary, then cook with the remaining 2 tbsp dressing in a skillet for 4 minutes on each side.
7. Divide the meat medallions into 4 serving plates.
8. Top them with their juices then add the tomatoes, cheese, and rice mixture.
9. Serve warm.

Nutrition: Calories: 357 kcal; Fats: 5 g; Carbohydrates: 39 g; Protein: 39 g

69
Crumbly Beef Meatballs

10 minutes

13 minutes

4

Ingredients

- 1 lb. ground beef
- 2 large eggs
- 1 ¼ cup low-carb breadcrumbs
- ¼ cup fresh parsley, chopped
- 1 tsp dried oregano
- ½ tsp ground nutmeg
- ¼ cup parmesan cheese, grated
- 1 small garlic clove, chopped
- A pinch of sea salt
- A pinch of pepper
- 1 tsp vegetable oil
- Cooking spray

Directions

1. Thoroughly mix the beef with the eggs, breadcrumbs, parsley, and the rest of the ingredients.
2. Make small meatballs out of this mixture and place them in the greased air fryer basket.
3. Place the basket inside the air fryer and close the lid.
4. Select the AIR FRY mode at 350°F for 13 minutes.
5. Toss the meatballs after 5 minutes. Serve and enjoy.

Nutrition: Calories: 357 kcal; Fats: 19 g; Carbohydrates: 21 g; Protein: 37 g

---

70
Easy Beef Meatballs

10 minutes

14 minutes

4

Ingredients

- 1 lb. ground beef
- 1 tsp garlic powder
- 1 egg, lightly beaten
- ½ onion, diced
- 1 tbsp fresh parsley, finely chopped
- 1 tsp paprika
- ¼ tsp pepper
- A pinch sea salt
- Cooking spray

Directions

1. Preheat the air fryer to 390°F. Spray the air fryer basket with cooking spray.
2. Add all the ingredients to the bowl and mix until well combined.
3. Make balls from the meat mixture and place them into the air fryer basket.
4. Cook meatballs for 14 minutes. Shake the basket 3–4 times while cooking. Serve and enjoy.

Nutrition: Calories: 230 kcal; Fats: 13 g; Carbohydrates: 2 g; Protein: 25 g

71
Fish Finger Sandwich

10 minutes

20 minutes

3

Ingredients

- 1 tbsp Greek yogurt
- 4 cod fillets, without skin
- 2 tbsp flour
- 5 tbsp whole-wheat breadcrumbs
- Kosher salt and pepper, to taste
- 10-12 capers
- ¾ cup frozen peas
- Lemon juice

Directions

1. Let the air fryer preheat to 200°C. Sprinkle kosher salt and pepper on the cod fillets, and coat in flour, then in breadcrumbs. Spray the fryer basket with oil. Put the cod fillets in the basket.
2. Cook for 15 minutes.
3. In the meantime, cook the peas in boiling water for a few minutes.
4. Take out of the water and blend with Greek yogurt, lemon juice, and capers until well combined. On a bun, add cooked fish with pea puree. Add lettuce and tomato.

Nutrition: Calories: 232 kcal; Fats: 2 g; Carbohydrates: 15 g; Protein: 37 g

72
Flavorful Pork Meatballs

10 minutes

10 minutes

2

Ingredients

- ½ lb. pork, ground
- 1 egg, lightly beaten
- 2 tbsp low-salt capers
- 2 garlic cloves, minced
- 2 tbsp fresh mint, chopped
- ½ tbsp cilantro, chopped
- 2 tsp red pepper flakes, crushed
- ½ tbsp light unsalted butter or margarine, melted
- A pinch of salt
- A pinch of black pepper
- Cooking spray

Directions

1. Preheat the air fryer to 395°F.
2. Put all of the ingredients in a mixing bowl and mix until well combined.
3. Spray the air fryer basket with cooking spray.
4. Make small balls from the meat mixture and place them in the air fryer basket.
5. Cook meatballs for 10 minutes. Shake the basket halfway through.
6. Serve and enjoy.

Nutrition: Calories: 297 kcal; Fats: 19 g; Carbohydrates: 23 g; Protein: 25 g

73
Garlic-Lime Shrimp Kebabs

 5 minutes   18 minutes   1

Ingredients

- 1 lime
- 1 cup raw shrimp
- ⅛ tsp salt
- 1 garlic clove, minced
- Black pepper, freshly ground

Directions

1. In water, let wooden skewers soak for 20 minutes.
2. Let the Air fryer preheat to 350°F.
3. In a bowl, mix shrimp, minced garlic, lime juice, salt, and pepper.
4. Thread the shrimp onto skewers.
5. Place the skewers in the air fryer and cook for 8 minutes, turning halfway through.
6. Top with cilantro and your favorite dip.

Nutrition: Calories: 128 kcal; Fats: 2 g; Carbohydrates: 5 g; Protein: 21 g

74
Green Beans and Lime Sauce

 13 minutes   10 minutes   2

Ingredients

- 1 lb. green beans, trimmed
- 2 tbsp ghee; melted
- 1 tbsp lime juice
- 1 tsp chili powder
- A pinch of salt and black pepper

Directions

1. Pre-heat an air fryer to 400°F
2. Take a bowl and mix the ghee with the rest of the ingredients except the green beans and whisk really well.
3. Mix the green beans with the lime sauce, and toss. Put them in your air fryer's basket and cook for 8 minutes. Serve right away.

Nutrition: Calories: 230 kcal; Fats: 10 g; Carbohydrates: 33 g; Protein: 9 g

75
Grilled Lemon Shrimps

🥣 1 hour	🕐 15 minutes	👥 3

Ingredients

- 1 lb. fresh shrimps, cleaned
- 1 tbsp fresh rosemary
- 4 tbsp extra-virgin olive oil
- 1 tsp garlic powder
- 2 tbsp lemon juice, freshly squeezed
- ½ tsp salt
- ½ tsp black pepper, freshly ground
- ½ tsp dried thyme, ground
- ½ tsp dried oregano, ground
- 1 organic lemon, sliced into wedges

Directions

1. Combine olive oil, garlic, lemon juice, salt, pepper, thyme, and oregano in a medium bowl and mix well.
2. Add the shrimp and coat evenly with the marinade mixture. Cover the bowl and chill for at least 1 hour to marinate the shrimps.
3. Preheat the grill to a medium-high temperature. Brush the grill grids with some oil.
4. Insert 2 to 3 shrimps on each skewer, brush with marinade, and grill for 3 minutes. Set and grill the other side for another 3 minutes. Transfer to a serving platter.
5. Serve warm with lemons wedges and sprinkle with chopped parsley.

Nutrition: Calories: 256 kcal; Fats: 18 g; Carbohydrates: 2.3 g; Protein: 37 g

76
Healthy Tuna Patties

 15 minutes   10 minutes   4

Ingredients

- ½ cup whole wheat breadcrumbs
- 4 cups fresh tuna, diced.
- Lemon zest
- 1 tbsp lemon juice
- 1 egg
- 3 tbsp parmesan cheese, grated
- 1 stalk of celery, chopped
- ½ tsp garlic powder
- ½ tsp dried herbs
- 3 tbsp onion, finely chopped
- Salt, to taste
- black pepper, freshly ground

Directions

1. Pre-heat the oven to 360°F. In a bowl, mix the lemon zest, breadcrumbs, salt, pepper, celery and eggs
2. Mix in the dried herbs, lemon juice, garlic powder, parmesan cheese, and onion.
3. Then add the tuna gently. Shape into patties, and if the mixture is too loose, cool in the refrigerator.
4. Cover the air fryer basket with air fryer baking paper. Spray the baking paper with cooking spray.
5. Spray the patties with oil and then cook them in the oven for 10 minutes, turning halfway through.
6. Serve with lemon slices and microgreens.

Nutrition: Calories: 300 kcal; Fats: 10 g; Carbohydrates: 5.75 g; Protein: 43 g

77
Herb-Crusted Salmon Fillets

10 minutes

10 minutes

4

Ingredients

- 16 oz. Atlantic salmon
- 2 tbsp chives, roughly chopped
- 2 tbsp parsley, chopped
- 1 cup whole-grain breadcrumbs
- ½ tsp garlic powder
- ½ tsp onion powder
- 1 tsp lemon peel, grated
- ¼ cup lemon juice
- ¼ tsp salt
- ½ tsp pepper
- Cooking spray

Directions

1. Preheat the oven to 400°F.
2. Line a baking tray with baking paper and spray it with some cooking oil.
3. Season the salmon fillets with pepper and salt.
4. Place the salmon on the baking tray, skin side down.
5. Put all the ingredients, except for the lemon juice, in a mixing bowl.
6. Combine well until it becomes a smooth mix.
7. Drizzle some lemon juice on the salmon fillets and spread the breadcrumb mixture on top.
8. Spray evenly with cooking spray, and bake for at least 10–15 minutes.
9. Serve hot.

Nutrition: Calories: 211 kcal; Fats: 7.75 g; Carbohydrates: 11 g; Protein: 25 g

78
Honey and Soy Glazed Salmon

10 minutes

7 minutes

2

Ingredients

- 2 fillets salmon
- 2 tbsp honey
- 1½ tbsp lime juice
- 2 tbsp soy sauce, low sodium
- 2 tbsp vegetable oil
- 2 tsp mustard
- 1 tbsp water

Directions

1. Put the honey, soy sauce, mustard, lime juice, and water in a medium bowl.
2. Pour vegetable oil into a non-stick skillet and bring to a high heat.
3. Roast the filets for at least 2 to 3 minutes.
4. Flip the filets over and continue roasting for another 2–3 minutes, until they becomes brown.
5. Transfer them onto a serving plate.
6. Add some honey glaze to the skillet and heat for 1 minute.
7. Pour the honey glaze over the salmon and serve hot.

Nutrition: Calories: 323 kcal; Fats: 21.5 g; Carbohydrates: 8.5 g; Protein: 25 g

79
Lemon Garlic Tilapia

10 minutes   **30 minutes**   **4**

Ingredients

- 4 fillets tilapia
- 1 tbsp olive oil
- 1 tbsp margarine
- 1 tbsp lemon juice
- ¼ tsp salt
- 1 tsp garlic salt
- 1 tsp dried parsley flakes
- ¼ tsp cayenne pepper
- Cooking spray

Directions

1. Pre-heat the oven to 400°F.
2. Spray nonstick cooking oil onto a baking tray.
3. Put the butter into a nonstick saucepan and melt it on low-medium heat.
4. Add some lemon juice, salt, olive oil, garlic powder, and parsley and sauté for 3-4 minutes.
5. Place the tilapia fillets in the baking tray and pour the liquid on top of the fillets.
6. Now sprinkle some cayenne pepper onto the fish.
7. Put in the oven and bake for about 12–13 minutes.
8. Flip over and cook for extra time.
9. Serve hot.

Nutrition: Calories: 147 kcal; Fats: 8 g; Carbohydrates: 0 g; Protein: 20 g

80
Sweet and Sour Tempeh

10 minutes   **30 minutes**   **2**

Ingredients

- 10 oz. tempeh
- 2 tbsp olive oil
- 2 tbsp soy sauce
- ¾ cup vegetable broth

FOR THE SAUCE:
- 1 tbsp cornstarch
- 15 oz. pineapple chunks
- 1 yellow onion, chopped
- 1 cup mushrooms, diced
- ¼ cup vinegar
- 1 tbsp erythritol
- 1 red bell pepper, chopped

Directions

1. To make this delightful dish, heat a large skillet over medium-high heat.
2. Next, add the tempeh along with the vegetable broth and soy sauce.
3. Braise the tempeh for about 8 to 10 minutes or until soft.
4. After that, remove the skillet from the heat and keep the braising liquid.
5. Now, take another skillet and spoon olive oil into it.
6. Heat it over medium heat and stir in the braised tempeh.
7. Cook the mixture for 3 minutes or until browned.
8. In the meantime, to make the sauce combine the reserved pineapple juice, vinegar, cornstarch, and brown sugar in a saucepan.
9. Heat the saucepan over medium heat and bring the mixture to a simmer while stirring continuously. Then, add the onion, mushrooms, and pepper and continue stirring until the mixture thickens.
10. Finally, lower the heat and stir in the braised tempeh and pineapple chunks and simmer for another 5 minutes.
11. **Serve it hot.**

Nutrition: Calories: 346 kcal; Fats: 22 g; Carbohydrates: 37 g; Protein: 30 g

81
Sweet Potato and Bell Pepper Soup

15 minutes   **35 minutes**   **4**

Ingredients

- 2 tbsp olive oil
- 1 medium white onion, chopped
- 1 red bell pepper, seeded and chopped
- 2 garlic cloves, minced
- 1 (1-inch) piece fresh ginger, grated
- 1 tsp dried rosemary, crushed
- 1 tsp dried thyme, crushed
- 1 tsp ground cinnamon
- ½ tsp cayenne pepper
- ½ cup tomato puree
- 1 tbsp maple syrup
- 3 cups low-fat vegetable broth
- 2 large sweet potatoes, peeled and chopped
- 2 tbsp fresh lemon juice
- Ground black pepper, as needed
- ¼ cup fresh cilantro, chopped

Directions

1. In a soup pan, heat the oil over medium heat and sauté the onion for about 5 minutes.
2. Add the bell pepper, garlic, ginger, dried herbs, cinnamon, and cayenne pepper; sauté for about 1 minute.
3. Stir in the tomato puree and maple syrup and cook for about 1 minute.
4. Stir in the sweet potatoes and broth and bring to a boil.
5. Simmer for about 10–15 minutes, stirring occasionally.
6. Remove from the heat and set aside to cool slightly.
7. In a blender, add the soup in 2 batches and pulse until smooth.
8. Return the soup to the same pan over medium-low heat and simmer for about 4–5 minutes or until heated completely.
9. Set in the lemon juice and black pepper and remove from the heat.
10. Serve hot with the garnishing of cilantro.

Nutrition: Calories: 348 kcal; Fats: 12.8 g; Carbohydrates: 54.5 g; Protein: 15.5 g

82
Sweet Potato and Kale Stew

15 minutes | 45 minutes | 3

Ingredients

- 2 tbsp olive oil
- 1 medium onion, chopped
- 1 medium sweet potato, peeled and cut into ½-inch-sized cubes
- 1 tsp fresh ginger, minced
- 4 garlic cloves, minced
- 1 Serrano pepper, seeded and chopped
- ¼ tsp red pepper flakes, crushed
- 1 tsp ground cumin
- ½ cup natural peanut butter
- 1 (6-oz.) can tomato paste
- 6 cups low-fat vegetable broth
- 3 cups fresh kale, tough ribs removed and chopped
- Salt and ground black pepper, as needed

Directions

1. In a heavy-bottomed saucepan, add olive oil and heat over medium heat.
2. Add onion and sauté for about 4–6 minutes.
3. Add sweet potato and cook for about 5–8 minutes.
4. Add ginger, garlic, serrano pepper, spices, and sauté for about 1 minute.
5. Add peanut butter and tomato paste and cook for about 2 minutes.
6. Add broth and bring to a boil.
7. Cover and cook for about 5 minutes.
8. Stir in kale, then adjust the heat to low.
9. Simmer for about 15 minutes.
10. Remove the pan of stew from the heat and set aside to cool slightly.
11. With a potato masher, blend half of the sweet potatoes.
12. Return the pan to a medium heat and simmer for about 2–3 minutes.
13. Season with salt and black pepper and serve hot.

Nutrition: Calories: 510 kcal; Fats: 33 g; Carbohydrates: 43 g; Fiber: 4.3 g; Protein: 18 g

83
Vegan Tofu Spinach Lasagna

 15 minutes   **30 minutes**   **3**

Ingredients

- 10 oz. lasagna
- 20 oz. bag of frozen spinach, thawed
- 14 oz. firm tofu
- 4 cups tomato sauce
- 1 tsp salt
- ¼ cup soy milk
- ½ tsp garlic powder
- 2 tbsp lime juice
- 10 oz. lasagna noodles
- 3 tbsp basil, fresh and chopped

Directions

1. First, place the tofu along with the soy milk, salt, garlic powder, basil, and lemon juice into a high-speed blender.
2. Blend for 1 to 2 minutes or until smooth.
3. After that, stir in the spinach and mash well.
4. Now, pour the tomato sauce into the pot.
5. Then, layer ⅓ of the lasagna noodles, the spinach mixture, and ⅓ of the tofu on top of it. Repeat the layers. Next, cook for 6 to 8 hours in the slow cooker.
6. Serve hot.

Nutrition: Calories: 820 kcal; Fats: 14 g; Carbohydrates: 133 g; Protein: 41 g

84
Wild Salmon Salad

10 minutes   **15 minutes**   **2**

Ingredients

- 2 medium-sized cucumbers, sliced
- A handful of iceberg lettuce, torn
- ¼ cup sweetcorn
- 1 large tomato, roughly chopped
- 8 oz. wild salmon, smoked and sliced
- 4 tbsp orange juice, freshly squeezed

DRESSING:
- 1 ¼ cup liquid yogurt, 2% fat
- 1 tbsp fresh mint, finely chopped
- 2 garlic cloves, crushed
- 1 tbsp sesame seeds

Directions

1. Combine vegetables in a large bowl. Drizzle with orange juice and top with salmon slices. Set aside.
2. In another bowl, whisk together yogurt, mint, crushed garlic, and sesame seeds.
3. Drizzle over the salad and toss to combine. Serve cold.

Nutrition: Calories: 275 kcal; Fats: 8 g; Carbohydrates: 25 g; Protein: 36,5 g

85
Spanish Chickpea Soup

10 minutes

4 hours 30 minutes

6

Ingredients

- 1 lb. dried chickpeas
- 6 chicken drumsticks
- 1 (4 oz.) piece Serrano ham, cubed
- 4 oz. Spanish-style chorizo, sliced
- 8 baby red potatoes, scrubbed and halved
- 1 large leek, halved and sliced
- 2 medium carrots, diced
- 2 stalks celery, chopped
- 3 large garlic cloves, minced
- 2 bay leaves
- 1 tbsp fresh oregano, chopped
- 1 tbsp smoked paprika
- ½ tsp saffron threads
- 6 cups chicken broth
- ½ medium cabbage, cut into 8 wedges
- Black pepper to taste
- ½ cup fresh parsley, chopped

Directions

1. Soak the chickpeas in cold water for 12 hours, then drain.
2. Place the chicken in a 6-quart slow cooker.
3. Add the chickpeas and the rest of the ingredients.
4. Cover and cook on high heat for almost 4 hours.
5. Add the cabbage and cook for 30 minutes.
6. Discard the bay leaves and remove the chicken from the bones.
7. Put the chicken back into the slow cooker and season with black pepper.
8. Garnish with parsley.
9. Serve warm.

Nutrition: Calories: 866 kcal; Fats: 21 g; Carbohydrates: 103 g; Protein: 57 g

86
Split Pea Soup

 10 minutes   2 hours 35 minutes   3

Ingredients

- 1 tbsp olive oil
- 2 cups onion, chopped
- 2 cups carrot, chopped
- 2 cups celery, chopped
- ½ tbsp garlic, minced
- 1 cup yellow split peas
- 1 cup green split peas
- 8 cups chicken broth
- 1 ½ tsp poultry seasoning blend
- 1 tsp salt

Directions

1. Sauté the garlic, celery, carrot, and onion with oil in a Dutch oven until soft.
2. Stir in the broth, split peas, seasoning and salt.
3. Cover, cook to a boil then reduce the heat to a simmer and cook for 2 ½ hours.
4. Puree this soup and serve warm.

Nutrition: Calories: 287 kcal; Fats: 12.8 g; Carbohydrates: 56 g; Protein: 9.6 g

---

87
Beef Brisket and Onion Sauce

 10 minutes   2 Hours   2

Ingredients

- ½ lb. beef brisket
- ½ cup. yellow onion, chopped
- ½ cup. celery, chopped
- ½ cup. carrot, chopped
- 4 cups water
- 8 earl gray tea bags
- Salt and black pepper, to taste

Directions

1. Preheat the air fryer to 300°F.
2. Put water in a pan that fits into the air fryer. Add the onions, celery, carrots, salt, and pepper. Stir and allow to simmer over medium-high heat.
3. Add the beef brisket, 8 earl grey tea bags, and stir. Put the pan into the air fryer then cook for 1 hour and 30 minutes.
4. Meanwhile, place a pan over medium-high heat, add vegetable oil, and heat until shimmering.
5. Add the sweet onion and sauté for 10 minutes.
6. Add the remaining sauce ingredients and cook for 10 minutes. Remove and discard the teabags.
7. Cut and serve the beef brisket with the onion sauce.

Nutrition: Calories: 287 kcal; Fats: 13 g; Carbohydrates: 7 g; Protein: 35 g

88
Perfect Chicken and Rice

 10 minutes
 25 minutes
 2

Ingredients

- 1 lb. chicken breasts, skinless and boneless
- 1 tsp olive oil
- 1 cup onion, diced
- 1 tsp garlic minced
- 4 carrots, peeled and sliced
- 1 tbsp Mediterranean spice mix
- 2 cups brown rice, rinsed
- 2 cups chicken stock
- Pepper, to taste
- Salt, to taste

Directions

1. Add oil to the inner pot of the Instant Pot and set the pot on "Sauté" mode. Add garlic and onion and sauté until the onion is softened.
2. Add stock, carrot, rice, and Mediterranean spice mix and stir well. Place chicken on top of the rice mixture and season with pepper and salt. Do not mix.
3. Seal the pot with a lid and select "Manual".
4. Set the timer for 20 minutes. Once done, allow the pressure to release naturally for 10 minutes then release the remaining pressure using quick release. Remove the lid.
5. Remove the chicken from the pot and shred using a fork. Return the shredded chicken to the pot and stir well. Serve and enjoy.

Nutrition: Calories: 621 kcal; Fats: 18 g; Carbohydrates: 58 g; Protein: 65 g

89
Chickpea Pepper Soup

 5 minutes

 40 minutes

 4

Ingredients

- 14 oz. dried chickpeas, soaked
- 2 large red bell peppers, finely chopped
- 2 small onions, peeled and finely chopped
- 2 large tomatoes, peeled and finely chopped
- 3 tbsp tomato paste
- A handful of fresh parsley, finely chopped
- 2 cups vegetable broth
- 3 tbsp extra virgin olive oil
- 1 tsp salt

Directions

1. Soak the chickpeas overnight. Rinse and drain. Place the chickpeas in a pot of boiling water and cook for 30 minutes. Remove from the heat and drain.
2. Wash the bell pepper and cut lengthwise in half. Remove the seeds and finely chop them. Set aside.
3. Preheat the oil in a large saucepan over medium-high temperature. Add onions and bell peppers. Cook for 5 minutes, or until tender. Add tomatoes, tomato paste, and parsley. Stir well and cook for 2 minutes. Now, add chickpeas and broth. Sprinkle with salt and stir again. Bring to a boil and reduce the heat to low. Cook for 30 minutes and remove from the heat.
4. Serve warm.

Nutrition: Calories: 387 kcal; Fats: 16 g; Carbohydrates: 57 g; Protein: 26 g

90
Arugula Risotto

 5 minutes   25 minutes   2

Ingredients

- 1 tbsp olive oil
- ½ cup yellow onion, chopped
- 1 cup quinoa, rinsed
- 1 garlic clove, minced
- 2 cups vegetable stock, low-sodium
- 2 cups arugula, chopped and stemmed
- 1 carrot, peeled and shredded
- ½ cup shiitake mushrooms, sliced
- ¼ tsp black pepper
- ¼ tsp sea salt, fine
- ¼ cup parmesan cheese, grated

Directions

1. Place a saucepan over medium heat and heat your oil.
2. Add onions and cook for 4 minutes until they are softened.
3. Next add your garlic and quinoa. Cook for 1 minute.
4. Stir in your stock and bring it to a boil.
5. Reduce it to simmer and cook for 12 minutes.
6. Add your arugula, mushrooms, and carrots, cooking for an additional 2 minutes.
7. Add salt, pepper, and cheese before serving.

Nutrition: Calories: 506 kcal; Carbohydrates: 72 g; Protein: 19 g; Fats: 16 g

91
Quinoa, Avocado, and Mango Salad

 15 minutes

 15 minutes

 4

Ingredients

- 2 cups quinoa, cooked
- 1½ cups fresh mango, peeled, pitted, and chopped
- 1 avocado, peeled, pitted, and chopped
- 1 cup sliced radishes
- 2 cups fresh baby arugula
- ¼ cup fresh mint leaves, chopped
- 2 garlic cloves, minced
- 2 tbsp fresh lemon juice
- 1½ tbsp olive oil
- Sea salt, as needed

Directions

1. Put all the ingredients in a glass salad bowl and gently stir to combine.
2. Refrigerate for about 1–2 hours before serving.

Nutrition: Calories: 437 kcal; Fats: 14 g; Carbohydrates: 66 g; Protein: 14 g

Chapter 3

DINNER

92
Paprika Baked Chicken Breasts

10 minutes | **10 minutes** | **3**

Ingredients

- 4–6 chicken breasts, boneless
- 1 tbsp olive oil
- 1 tbsp paprika
- 1 tbsp erythritol
- 1 tsp ground coriander
- ½ tsp garlic powder
- ¼ tsp cayenne pepper
- ½ tsp ground black pepper
- Salt to taste

Directions

1. Preheat the oven to 400°F.
2. Prepare a baking sheet and line it with parchment paper.
3. Mix coriander, paprika, salt, sugar, black pepper, garlic powder, and cayenne pepper in a bowl.
4. Drizzle the chicken breasts with oil and rub with the spice mixture.
5. Refrigerate for about 15 minutes.
6. Place on the baking sheet and cook for 30 minutes. Let it cool before serving.

Nutrition: Calories: 366 kcal; Fats: 11 g; Carbohydrates: 13 g; Protein: 54 g

93
Walnut and Beet Salad

10 minutes | **12 minutes** | **2**

Ingredients

- 1 oz. Gruyere cheese
- 1 cup arugula/rocket
- 7 oz. fresh beets
- 2 tsp olive oil
- 2 cups baby spinach
- ½ cup walnuts

Directions

1. Peel the fresh beets and chop them into pieces.
2. Put the olive oil into a pan and heat on a medium heat.
3. Put the beets into the pan and fry for about 10 minutes.
4. Once cooked, allow them to cool. Combine all salad ingredients in a bowl and serve.

Nutrition: Calories: 407 kcal; Fats: 37 g; Carbohydrates: 12 g; Protein: 11 g

94
Asparagus Avocado Soup

 10 minutes   20 minutes   2

Ingredients

- 1 avocado, peeled, pitted, and cubed
- 12 oz. asparagus
- ½ tsp ground black pepper
- 1 tsp garlic powder
- 1 tsp sea salt
- 2 tbsp olive oil
- ½ lemon, juiced
- 2 cups vegetable stock

Directions

1. Switch on the air fryer, insert the fryer basket, grease it with olive oil and close.
2. Set the fryer to 425°F, and preheat for 5 minutes.
3. Meanwhile, place the asparagus in a shallow dish, drizzle with 1 tbsp oil, sprinkle with garlic powder, salt, and black pepper, and toss until well mixed.
4. Add the asparagus to the fryer and cook for 10 minutes until nicely golden and roasted, shaking halfway through the frying.
5. When the air fryer beeps, open its lid and transfer asparagus to a food processor.
6. Add the remaining ingredients to the food processor and pulse until well combined and smooth.
7. Tip the soup into a saucepan, pour in water if the soup is too thick, and heat over medium-low heat for 5 minutes until thoroughly heated.
8. Ladle soup into bowls and serve.

Nutrition: Calories: 301 kcal; Fats: 27 g Carbohydrates: 16 g; Protein: 6 g

95
Broccoli Gorgonzola Soup

 **10 minutes**   **2 hours**   **3**

Ingredients

- 10 oz. low-fat cheese, crumbled
- 1 cup broccoli, finely chopped
- 1 tbsp olive oil
- ½ cup full-fat milk
- ½ cup vegetable broth
- 1 tbsp parsley, finely chopped
- ½ tsp salt
- ¼ tsp ground black pepper

Directions

1. Wash the broccoli under cold running water. Drain and chop into bite-sized pieces. Set aside.
2. Grease the bottom of a deep pot with olive oil.
3. Add all ingredients and 3 cups of water. Mix well with a kitchen whisk until fully combined.
4. Cover with a lid and cook for 2 hours at low temperature.
5. Remove from the heat and sprinkle with some fresh parsley for extra taste.
6. Stir in one tbsp of Greek yogurt before serving if you like.

Nutrition: Calories: 407 kcal; Fats: 12 g; Carbohydrates: 8 g; Protein: 22 g

96
Cheesy Cauliflower Soup

 10 minutes    **45 minutes**   **3**

Ingredients

- 3 tbsp olive oil
- ¾ cup onions, finely chopped
- 5 cups chicken broth
- 1 cup water
- 1 medium cauliflower, cut into florets
- ⅓ tsp rosemary
- ⅛ tsp thyme
- ¼ tsp black pepper
- 2 tbsp butter, melted
- ¼ cup whole flour
- 1 cup cheddar cheese, shredded

Directions

1. In a large saucepan, heat oil; add the onions and cook over medium heat until softened, for about 5 minutes.
2. Add broth, water, cauliflower, rosemary, thyme, and pepper. Cover; cook over low heat for 30 minutes, or until the cauliflower is tender. Remove from the heat.
3. Using a potato masher, mash the cauliflower mixture until the cauliflower is broken into small pieces; return to the heat.
4. In a small bowl, combine the melted butter and flour. Mix well, then add to the soup, cooking over low heat and stirring until the soup is thickened to the desired consistency.
5. Add cheese, one cup at a time, stirring until it is melted. Serve.

Nutrition: Calories: 411 kcal; Fats: 22 g; Carbohydrates: 19 g; Protein: 19 g

97
Chicken Bisque

10 minutes

57 minutes

3

Ingredients

- 2 lb. chicken, cut into pieces
- 8 oz. basmati rice
- 10 oz. chicken stock
- 6 oz. dry white wine
- ½ large orange, cut into wedges
- 1 tsp fresh thyme, chopped
- 2 oz. black olives
- Salt and black pepper, to taste
- 2 large red peppers, sliced
- 2 medium onions, sliced
- 3 tbsp olive oil
- 5 oz. chorizo sausage, skinned and diced
- 2 oz. sun-dried tomatoes
- 2 large garlic cloves, chopped
- 1 tbsp sun-dried tomato paste
- ½ tsp hot paprika

Directions

1. Start by seasoning the chicken with salt and black pepper.
2. Heat some oil in a pan then sear the chicken pieces until golden brown.
3. Transfer the chicken onto a plate lined with kitchen towel.
4. Stir the peppers and onion into the hot oil.
5. Sauté for 5 minutes then add the tomatoes, garlic, and chorizo.
6. Stir for 2 minutes then toss in the rice.
7. Add the sun-dried tomato paste, paprika, and thyme.
8. Pour in the wine and stock then add seasoning.
9. Let the mixture cook until it reaches a simmer.
10. Spread the orange wedges and olives over the chicken.
11. Cover the chicken and cook for 50 minutes on low heat.
12. Serve warm.

Nutrition: Calories: 638 kcal; Fats: 23 g; Carbohydrates: 58 g; Protein: 64 g

98
Chicken Kofta

15 minutes	27 minutes	4

Ingredients

- 2 medium yellow onions, chopped
- 4 garlic cloves, chopped
- ¼ cup olive oil + 2 tbsp
- 2 tsp salt
- 2 tsp ground cumin
- 1 tsp ground coriander
- ½ tsp red pepper flakes
- 2 cups parsley leaves
- 1 cup mint leaves
- 2 lb. chicken, ground

Directions

1. Preheat your oven to 425°F.
2. Place the garlic and yellow onions in a food processor and finely chop.
3. Pour some oil into a large skillet over medium-high heat.
4. Stir in the salt and onion-garlic mixture.
5. Stir for 10 minutes, then add the coriander, red pepper, and cumin.
6. Stir for 1 minute then add the chopped mint and parsley.
7. Stir in the chicken and remaining salt.
8. Mix well and divide the mixture into 16 parts.
9. Roll the parts into balls then press them into patties.
10. Place the patties onto a baking sheet and bake for 8 minutes on each side in the oven.
11. Serve warm.

Nutrition: Calories: 351 kcal; Fats: 17 g; Carbohydrates: 9 g; Protein: 44 g

99
Chicken with Tomatoes, Olives, and Capers

 10 minutes   11 minutes   1

Ingredients

- 1 chicken breast, boneless
- ¼ cup seasoned flour, for dusting
- 1 tbsp olive oil
- 1 large ripe tomato, chopped
- 2 tsp capers
- A handful olives
- 1 splash white wine
- A handful of parsley and chives, chopped

Directions

1. Slice the chicken breast into 2 halves and spread it open like a book.
2. Take a rolling pin and bash the meat to flatten it.
3. Coat the chicken well with seasoned flour.
4. Sear the coated chicken in heated oil in a pan for 4 minutes on each side until golden and crispy.
5. Remove the chicken from the cooking pan and set it aside, keeping it warm.
6. Add the wine, olives, tomato, and capers to the same pan.
7. Adjust the seasoning then boil the sauce for 2–3 minutes.
8. Spoon this sauce over the chicken and garnish it with herbs.
9. Enjoy with steamed potatoes.

Nutrition: Calories: 543 kcal; Fats: 27 g; Carbohydrates: 30 g; Protein: 35 g

100
Creamy Chicken Vegetable Soup

15 minutes

45 minutes

3

Ingredients

- 2 tbsp olive oil
- ½ cup onions, finely chopped
- ½ cup carrots, thinly sliced or shredded
- ½ cup potatoes, diced
- ½ cup green beans
- ½ cup peas
- 1 cup chicken, finely chopped
- 1 (14-oz.) can chicken broth
- ¼ tsp black pepper
- 1¼ cups milk
- 1 (10¾-oz.) can cream of celery soup
- 1 (10¾-oz.) can cream of cheddar cheese soup

Directions

1. In a large saucepan, heat the oil.
2. Add onions and carrots. Cook and stir until softened, about 5 minutes.
3. Add potatoes, green beans, peas, chicken, broth, and pepper. Cover, and cook over low heat for 1½ hours, or until vegetables are soft; stir occasionally.
4. Add milk, celery soup, and cheddar cheese soup; stir and continue cooking until heated throughout.

Nutrition: Calories: 303 kcal; Fats: 13 g; Carbohydrates: 21 g; Protein: 21 g

101
Creamy Leek Soup

 **15 minutes**   **20 minutes**   **3**

Ingredients

- 1 cup leeks, chopped
- 1 medium-sized potato
- 1 large carrot, chopped
- 1 cup chicken stock, unsalted
- 1 cup milk, low-fat
- 1 cup spinach, finely chopped
- 1 tbsp parsley, finely chopped
- ¼ tsp ground black pepper

Directions

1. Wash and prepare the vegetables. Place the leeks, spinach, and celery in a pot of boiling water. Cook for 3 minutes and remove from the heat. Drain well and set aside.
2. Place the potato in a pot of boiling water and cook for 5 minutes, or until slightly tender. Remove from the heat and drain well. Set aside.
3. Now, combine the leeks, potato, carrot, and spinach in a heavy-bottomed pot.
4. Pour in the chicken stock and milk. Sprinkle with pepper and parsley. Bring it to a boil and then reduce the heat to low.
5. Simmer for 15 minutes and remove from the heat. Transfer all to a food processor and pulse until creamy and pureed. Return to the pot and reheat.
6. Serve warm.

Nutrition: Calories: 162 kcal; Fats: 3.6 g; Carbohydrates: 27 g; Protein: 9 g

102
Creamy Wild Asparagus Soup

10 minutes

20 minutes

3

Ingredients

- 2 lb. fresh wild asparagus, trimmed
- 2 small onions, peeled and finely chopped
- 1 cup heavy cream
- 4 cups vegetable broth
- 2 tbsp butter
- 1 tbsp vegetable oil
- ½ tsp salt
- ½ tsp dried oregano
- ½ tsp cayenne pepper

Directions

1. Rinse and drain the asparagus. Cut into about one-inch thick pieces. Set aside.
2. Melt the butter in a large skillet and add oil. Heat up and add the onions. Cook until translucent.
3. Now add the trimmed asparagus, oregano, salt, and cayenne pepper. Stir well and continue to cook until the asparagus has softened.
4. Add the vegetable broth and mix well to combine. Cook for 15 minutes, stirring occasionally.
5. Whisk in 1 cup of heavy cream and serve.

Nutrition: Calories: 136 kcal; Fats: 4.3 g; Carbohydrates: 20 g; Protein: 9.6 g

103
Delicious Chicken Casserole

10 minutes   20 minutes   2

Ingredients

- 1 lb. chicken breasts, skinless, boneless, and cubed
- 2 tsp paprika
- 3 tbsp tomato paste
- 1 cup chicken stock
- 4 tomatoes, chopped
- 1 small eggplant, chopped
- 1 tbsp Italian seasoning
- 2 bell pepper, sliced
- 1 onion, sliced
- 1 tbsp garlic, minced
- 1 tbsp olive oil
- Pepper, to taste
- Salt, to taste

Directions

1. Add oil to the inner pot of the Instant Pot and set the pot on "Sauté" mode. Season the chicken with pepper and salt and add to the Instant Pot. Cook the chicken until lightly golden brown.
2. Remove the chicken from the pot and place on a plate. Add garlic and onion and sauté until the onion is softened, about 3–5 minutes.
3. Return the chicken to the pot. Pour the remaining ingredients over the chicken and stir well. Seal the pot with a lid and cook on high for 10 minutes.
4. Once done, release the pressure using quick release. Remove the lid. Stir well and serve.

Nutrition: Calories: 528 kcal; Fats: 14 g; Carbohydrates: 45 g; Protein: 66 g

104
Easy Beef Kofta

10 minutes   10 minutes   4

Ingredients

- 2 lb. beef, ground
- 4 garlic cloves, minced
- 1 onion, minced
- 2 tsp cumin
- 1 cup fresh parsley, chopped
- ¼ tsp pepper
- 1 tsp salt

Directions

1. Add all the listed ingredients to the mixing bowl and mix until combined.
2. Roll the meat mixture into the kebab shapes and cook in a hot pan for 4–6 minutes on each side or until cooked.
3. Serve and enjoy.

Nutrition: Calories: 476kcal; Fats: 26 g; Carbohydrates: 6 g; Protein: 50 g

105
Lentils and Quinoa Stew

15 minutes   **33 minutes**   **3**

Ingredients

- 1 tbsp extra-virgin olive oil
- 3 carrots, peeled and chopped
- 3 celery stalks, chopped
- 1 yellow onion, chopped
- 4 garlic cloves, minced
- 4 cups fresh tomatoes, chopped
- 1 cup red lentils, rinsed and drained
- ½ cup quinoa, dried, rinsed and drained
- 1½ tsp ground cumin
- 1 tsp red chili powder
- 5 cups low-fat vegetable broth
- 2 cups fresh spinach, chopped

Directions

1. Pour olive oil into a heavy-bottomed saucepan and heat over a medium heat.
2. Add the celery, onion, and carrot, and cook for about 8 minutes, stirring frequently.
3. Add the garlic and sauté for about 1 minute.
4. Add the remaining ingredients (except spinach) and bring to a boil.
5. Now adjust the heat to low and simmer, covered, for about 20 minutes.
6. Stir in the spinach and simmer for about 3–4 minutes. Serve hot.

Nutrition: Calories: 359 kcal; Fats: 8 g; Carbohydrates: 67g; Protein: 27 g; **Sugar:** 7.1 g

106
Marinated Tuna

 2 hours 10 minutes   **15 minutes**   **4**

Ingredients

- 2 lb. tuna steaks, boneless
- ¼ cup fresh coriander, chopped
- 2 garlic cloves, minced
- 2 tbsp lemon juice
- ½ cup olive oil
- ½ tsp smoked paprika
- ½ tsp ground cumin
- ½ tsp ground chili pepper
- ½ tsp salt
- ¼ tsp ground black pepper

Directions

1. Add the coriander, garlic, paprika, cumin, chili, and lemon juice to a food processor and pulse to combine. Gradually add in the oil and mix the ingredients until they form a smooth mixture.
2. Transfer the mixture into a bowl, add the fish and gently toss to coat the fish evenly with sauce. Chill for at least 2 hours to allow the flavors to penetrate the fish.
3. Remove the fish from the chiller and preheat the grill. Lightly brush the grid with oil, place the fish on the grid, and grill for about 3 to 4 minutes on each side.
4. Remove the fish from the grill, transfer to a serving plate and serve with lemon wedges or some vegetables.

Nutrition: Calories: 433 kcal; Fats: 29 g; Carbohydrates: 2 g; Protein: 55 g

107
Mom's Sloppy Joes

10 minutes

30 minutes

4

Ingredients

- Nonstick cooking spray
- 1½ lb. supreme lean ground beef
- 1 cup onion, chopped
- 1 cup celery, chopped
- 1 (8-oz.) can tomato sauce
- ⅓ cup catsup (free of high-fructose corn syrup)
- 2 tbsp white vinegar
- 2 tbsp Worcestershire sauce
- 2 tbsp Dijon mustard
- 1 tbsp erythritol

Directions

1. Spray a large skillet with the cooking spray and place it over a medium heat. Add the beef and brown until it is no longer pink, for about 10 minutes. Drain off any grease.
2. Mix in the onion and celery and cook for 2 to 3 minutes.
3. Stir in the tomato sauce, catsup, vinegar, Worcestershire sauce, mustard, and brown sugar. Bring the liquid to a simmer and reduce the heat to low. Cook for 15 minutes, or until the sauce has thickened.
4. Spoon about ¾ cup of the sloppy Joe mixture onto each plate and serve.

Nutrition Per Serving (¾ cup): Calories: 250 kcal; Fats: 5 g; Protein: 25 g; Carbohydrates: 18 g

108
Mushroom and Corn Curry

 15 minutes

 20 minutes

 4

Ingredients

- 2 cups tomatoes, chopped
- 1 green chili, chopped
- 1 tsp fresh ginger, chopped
- ¼ cup cashews
- 2 tbsp olive oil
- ½ tsp cumin seeds
- ¼ tsp ground coriander
- ¼ tsp ground turmeric
- ¼ tsp red chili powder
- 1½ cups fresh shiitake mushrooms, sliced
- 1½ cups fresh button mushrooms, sliced
- 1 cup corn kernels, frozen
- 1¼ cups water
- ¼ cup coconut milk, unsweetened

Directions

1. In a food processor, put tomatoes, green chili, ginger, and cashews, and pulse until a smooth paste forms.
2. In a pan, heat oil over a medium heat and sauté cumin seeds for about 1 minute.
3. Add spices and sauté for about 1 minute.
4. Add tomato paste and cook for about 5 minutes.
5. Stir in the mushrooms, corn, water, and coconut milk, and cook for about 10-12 minutes, stirring occasionally.
6. Serve hot.

Nutrition: Calories: 170 kcal; Fats: 11 g; Carbohydrates: 14 g; Protein: 3.75 g

109
One-Pan Pork Chops with Apples and Red Onion

10 minutes   25 minutes   4

Ingredients

- 4 thin pork chops, boneless, center-cut
- 2 small apples, thinly sliced
- 1 small red onion, thinly sliced
- 1 cup low-sodium chicken broth
- 1 tsp Dijon mustard
- 1 tsp dried sage
- 1 tsp dried thyme
- 1 tsp rosemary
- A pinch of black pepper
- Cooking spray

Directions

1. Place a large non-stick frying pan over high heat and coat with cooking spray.
2. When the oil is hot, add the pork chops and black pepper, and reduce the heat to medium.
3. Sear the chops for 3 minutes on one side, flip, and sear the other side for 3 minutes. Set the chops aside.
4. Coat the same pan with cooking spray, if needed. Add the apples and onion, and cook for 5 minutes or until tender, stirring frequently.
5. While the apples and onion cook, mix the broth and Dijon mustard in a small bowl.
6. Add the sage, rosemary, and thyme to the pan and stir to coat the onion and apples.
7. Stir in the broth mixture and return the pork chops to the pan.
8. Cover and simmer for 10-15 minutes.
9. Let the pork chops rest for 2 minutes before cutting.

Nutrition: Calories: 369 kcal; Fats: 15 g; Carbohydrates: 38 g; Protein: 35 g

110
Pumpkin and Black Beans Soup

15 minutes | **15 minutes** | **3**

Ingredients

- 2 tbsp olive oil
- 1 medium white onion, chopped
- 4 garlic cloves, minced
- 1 tbsp ground cumin
- 1 tsp red chili powder
- Ground black pepper, as needed
- 2 cans black beans, rinsed and drained thoroughly
- 16 oz. canned sugar-free pumpkin puree
- 1 cup fresh tomatoes, chopped finely
- 2 cups low-fat chicken broth
- ¼ cup fat-free plain Greek yogurt
- ¼ cup fresh cilantro, chopped

Directions

1. In a soup pan, heat the oil over medium heat and sauté the onion for about 4–5 minutes.
2. Add the garlic, cumin, chili powder, and black pepper; sauté for about 1 minute.
3. Add the black beans, pumpkin, tomatoes, and broth, and stir to combine.
4. Now adjust the heat to medium-high and bring to a boil.
5. Then, adjust the heat to low and simmer, uncovered, for about 25 minutes, stirring occasionally.
6. Remove from the heat and stir in the yogurt.
7. With an immersion blender, blend the soup until smooth.
8. Serve hot with the garnish of cilantro.

Nutrition: Calories: 461 kcal; Fats: 10 g; Carbohydrates: 66 g; Protein: 23 g

111
Roasted Veggie Bowl

 25 min   5 min   1

Ingredients

- ¼ medium white onion, peeled and sliced ¼-inch thick
- ½ medium green bell pepper, seeded and sliced ¼-inch thick
- 1 cup broccoli florets
- 1 cup Brussels sprouts, quartered
- ½ cup cauliflower florets
- 1 tbsp coconut oil
- ½ tsp garlic powder.
- ½ tsp cumin
- 2 tsp chili powder

Directions

1. Toss all ingredients together in a large bowl until the vegetables are fully coated with oil and seasoning. Pour the vegetables into the air fryer basket.
2. Adjust the temperature to 360°F and set the timer for 15 minutes.
3. Shake 2-or 3-times during cooking. Serve warm.

Nutrition: Calories: 196 kcal; Fats: 7 g; Carbohydrates: 26 g; Protein: 11 g

112
Shrimp Egg Rolls

 20 minutes   **20 minutes**   **3**

Ingredients

- 2-3 garlic cloves, minced
- 12-14 egg roll wrappers
- 4 cups raw shrimp, roughly chopped, peeled, and deveined.
- 3 cups coleslaw mix
- 1 ½ tsp sesame oil
- 1 tbsp soy sauce
- 1 tsp fish sauce
- Salt and pepper, to taste
- ½ tsp ginger, grated
- 2 green onions, chopped
- 1 cup of water

Directions

1. In a skillet, add the shrimp with garlic, kosher salt, and pepper, spray with cooking oil and sauté until the shrimp is pink. Set it aside.
2. In a bowl, add coleslaw mix, cooked shrimp, green onions, fish sauce, soy sauce, sesame oil, and ginger. Mix well.
3. Add 2 tbsp of filling to each wrapper, and seal tightly with water.
4. With cooking oil, spray the air fryer basket. Put the egg rolls in a single layer in the basket. Spray with cooking oil.
5. Cook for 7 minutes at 400°F. Flip the rolls, then cook for 5 minutes more. Serve with a microgreen salad.

Nutrition: Calories: 366 kcal; Fats: 2.3 g; Carbohydrates: 58 g; Protein: 29 g

113
Slow Cooker Pork with Red Peppers and Pineapple

10 minutes | **5 hours** | **4**

Ingredients

- 1 ½ lb. pork tenderloin, boneless
- ¼ cup low-sodium soy sauce
- ½ lemon, juiced
- 1 tsp garlic powder
- 1 tsp ground cumin
- ½ tsp cayenne pepper
- ¼ tsp ground coriander
- ½ tsp fresh rosemary, minced
- ½ tsp fresh sage, minced
- 2 red bell peppers, thinly sliced
- 1 (20-oz.) can pineapple chunks, unsweetened

Directions

1. In a small bowl, mix the soy sauce, lemon juice, garlic powder, cumin, cayenne pepper, rosemary, sage, and coriander.
2. Place the pork tenderloin in the slow cooker and add the red bell pepper slices.
3. Cover with the pineapple chunks and their juices. Add the soy sauce mixture.
4. Cover the slow cooker, turn on LOW and cook for about 5 hours.
5. Shred the pork with a fork and cook on LOW for an additional 20 minutes.

Nutrition: Calories: 195 kcal; Fats: 2.75 g; Carbohydrates: 17 g; Protein: 25 g

114
Sushi Roll

1 hour 30 minutes | **10 minutes** | **3**

Ingredients

For the Kale Salad:

- ½ tsp rice vinegar
- 1 and ½ cups chopped kale.
- ⅛ tsp garlic powder
- 1 tbsp sesame seeds
- ¾ tsp toasted sesame oil
- ¼ tsp ground ginger
- ¾ tsp Sriracha Mayo
- Soy sauce

For the Sushi rolls

- ½ avocado, sliced.
- 1 cup sushi rice, cooked, cooled
- ½ cup whole wheat breadcrumbs
- 3 sheets sushi

Directions

1. In a bowl, add vinegar, garlic powder, kale, soy sauce, sesame oil, and ground ginger. With your hands, mix with sesame seeds and set them aside.
2. Lay a sheet of sushi on a flat surface. With damp fingertips, add a tbsp of rice, and spread it on the sheet. Cover the sheet with rice leaving a half-inch space at one end.
3. Add kale salad with avocado slices. Roll up the sushi, and use water if needed. Add the breadcrumbs to a bowl. Coat the sushi roll with Sriracha Mayo, then in breadcrumbs.
4. Add the rolls to the air fryer. Cook for ten minutes at 390°F, and shake the basket halfway through. Take them out of the fryer, and let them cool. Next cut them with a sharp knife. Serve with soy sauce.

Nutrition: Calories: 255 kcal; Fats: 11 g; Carbohydrates: 33 g; Protein: 7 g

115
Seasoned Pork Chops

 10 minutes

 4 hours

 2

Ingredients

- 4 pork chops
- 2 garlic cloves, minced
- 1 cup chicken broth
- 1 tbsp poultry seasoning
- ¼ cup olive oil
- Pepper and salt, to taste

Directions

1. In a bowl, whisk together olive oil, poultry seasoning, garlic, broth, pepper, and salt.
2. Pour olive oil mixture into the slow cooker, then place pork chops in the pot.
3. Cook on high for 4 hours.
4. Serve and enjoy.

Nutrition: Calories: 504kcal; Fats: 40 g; Carbohydrates: 1 g; Protein: 29 g

116
Slow Cooker Chicken Chili

 10 minutes

 8 hours

 8-10

Ingredients

- ½ tsp garlic, minced
- ½ cup kidney beans
- Nonstick spray
- 1 bell pepper, diced
- 2 lb. chicken meat
- 3 tbsp ground cumin
- 3 tbsp chili powder
- 1 tsp dried oregano
- 1 cup tomato puree
- ½ cup celery, finely chopped
- ½ cup onions, chopped
- 2 cups water

Directions

1. Put all the ingredients, except for the chicken, into a slow cooker and cook for 8 hours.
2. Cook the chicken pieces until they turn light brown.
3. Serve the chicken on the bean mixture. You can serve with Greek yogurt if you like.

Nutrition: Calories: 133 kcal; Fats: 2 g; Carbohydrates: 8 g; Protein: 23 g

117
Spinach Potato Cream Soup

 15 minutes   35 minutes   3

Ingredients

- 1 lb. fresh spinach, chopped
- 2 medium-sized potatoes, chopped
- 3 tbsp fresh parsley, chopped
- 1 small onion, finely chopped
- 2 tbsp olive oil
- 2 tbsp all-purpose flour
- 2 cups chicken broth
- 1 cup cream cheese
- ½ tsp cayenne pepper
- 1 tsp salt
- ¼ tsp ground black pepper

Directions

1. Rinse the spinach thoroughly under cold running water. Drain well and chop into small pieces. Set aside.
2. Peel the potatoes and chop them into bite-sized pieces. Set aside.
3. Place the spinach in a pot of boiling water and cook for 3 minutes, or until tender. Remove from the heat and drain.
4. Place the potatoes in a pot of boiling water and sprinkle them with some salt.
5. Let them boil and cook for 10 minutes. Remove from the heat and drain.
6. Set aside.
7. Preheat the oil in a large skillet over a medium-high temperature. Add onion and stir-fry until translucent. Stir in the flour, cayenne pepper, and 1 tbsp of water. Cook for 1 minute, stirring constantly. Remove from the heat.
8. In a large heavy-bottomed pot, pour chicken broth and 1 cup of water. Bring it to a boil over a medium-high temperature.
9. Add spinach and potatoes and sprinkle with pepper. Cook for 10 minutes, and reduce the heat to low. Cook for another 5 minutes and then stir in the sour cream and parsley.
10. Now, transfer all to a food processor in a few batches. Pulse until creamy and pureed. Transfer to the pot and stir in the flour mixture. Cook for 2 more minutes.
11. Remove from the heat and set aside to cool for a while before serving.

Nutrition: Calories: 256 kcal; Fats: 23 g; Carbohydrates: 36 g; Protein: 8 g

118
Sweet Potato Chips

 5 minutes   10 minutes   1

Ingredients

- 2 large sweet potatoes
- 15 ml. olive oil
- 10 g salt
- 2 g black pepper
- 2 g paprika
- 2 g garlic powder
- 2 g onion powder

Directions

1. Cut the sweet potatoes into strips 25 mm. thick.
2. Preheat the air fryer to 400°F.
3. Add the cut sweet potatoes to a large bowl and mix with the oil until the potatoes are all evenly coated.
4. Sprinkle salt, black pepper, paprika, garlic powder, and onion powder. Mix well.
5. Place the French fries in the preheated baskets and cook for 10 minutes. Be sure to shake the baskets halfway through cooking.

Nutrition: Calories: 449 kcal; Fats: 21 g Carbohydrates: 50 g; Protein: 5 g

119
Tender Chicken and Mushrooms

10 minutes   **21 minutes**   **2**

Ingredients

- 1 lb. chicken breasts, skinless, boneless, and cut into 1-inch pieces
- ¼ cup olives, sliced
- 2 oz. feta cheese, crumbled
- ¼ cup sherry
- 1 cup chicken broth
- 1 tsp Italian seasoning
- 12 oz. mushrooms, sliced
- 2 celery stalks, diced
- 1 tsp garlic, minced
- ½ cup onion, chopped
- 2 tbsp olive oil
- Pepper, to taste
- Salt, to taste

Directions

1. Add oil to the inner pot of the Instant Pot and set the pot on "Sauté" mode. Add mushrooms, celery, garlic, onion, and sauté for 5–7 minutes.
2. Add chicken, Italian seasoning, pepper, and salt and stir well and cook for 4 minutes. Add sherry and broth and stir well. Seal the pot with a lid and cook on high for 10 minutes.
3. Once done, allow the pressure to release naturally for 10 minutes then release the remaining using quick release. Remove the lid. Add olives and feta cheese and stir well. Serve and enjoy.

Nutrition: Calories: 663 kcal; Fats: 26 g; Carbohydrates: 7 g; Protein: 69 g

120
Tomato Pork Chops

10 minutes · **6 hours** · **2**

Ingredients

- 4 pork chops, bone-in
- 1 tbsp garlic, minced
- ½ small onion, chopped
- 6 oz. can tomato paste
- 1 bell pepper, chopped
- ¼ tsp red pepper flakes
- 1 tsp Worcestershire sauce
- 1 tbsp dried Italian seasoning
- 14 ½ oz. can of chopped tomatoes
- 2 tsp olive oil
- ¼ tsp pepper
- 1 tsp kosher salt

Directions

1. Heat oil in a pan over medium heat. Season pork chops with pepper and salt. Sear the pork chops in the pan until brown on both sides.
2. Transfer the pork chops to the pot. Add the remaining ingredients to the pork chops. Cook on low heat for 6 hours. Serve and enjoy.

Nutrition: Calories: 415kcal; Fats: 19 g; Carbohydrates: 27 g; Protein: 33 g

121
Tomato Rotisserie

15 minutes · **4 minutes** · **4**

Ingredients

- 1 lb. Rotisserie chicken
- 15 petite tomatoes, diced
- 9 tortillas
- 1 cup cheese, shredded
- ½ cup plain Greek yogurt
- 1 avocado
- 1 lime

Directions

1. Shred your chicken, then put it in a microwave-safe bowl. Add tomatoes and the seasoning to the bowl and mix.
2. Microwave for 4 minutes on high. Fill the tortillas with the chicken. Top with the remaining ingredients and a squeeze of lime.

Nutrition: Calories: 650 kcal; Fats: 30 g Carbohydrates: 54 g; Protein: 38 g

122
Vegan Edamame Quinoa Collard Wraps

5 minutes

15 minutes

1

Ingredients

FOR THE WRAP:
- 2–3 collard leaves
- ¼ cup carrot, grated
- ¼ cup cucumber, sliced
- ¼ red bell pepper, in thin strips
- ¼ orange bell pepper, in thin strips
- ⅓ cup quinoa, cooked
- ⅓ cup of frozen edamame beans, shelled and defrosted

FOR THE DRESSING:
- 3 tbsp fresh ginger root, peeled and chopped
- 1 cup chickpeas, cooked
- 1 garlic clove
- 4 tbsp rice vinegar
- 2 tbsp low-sodium tamari/ coconut aminos
- 2 tbsp lime juice
- ¼ cup water
- Few pinches chili flakes
- 1 pack stevia

Directions

1. For the dressing, combine all the ingredients and purée in a food processor until smooth.
2. Pour into a little jar or tub and set aside.
3. Place the collard leaves on a flat surface, covering one another to create a tighter tie.
4. Take 1 tbsp of ginger dressing and blend it up with the prepared quinoa.
5. Spoon the prepared quinoa onto the leaves and shape a simple horizontal line at the closest end.
6. Add all the veggie fillings left over.
7. Drizzle around 1 tbsp of the ginger dressing on top, then fold the cover's sides inwards.
8. Pull the leaves over the filling, then turn it upside down to seal it up.

Nutrition: Calories: 475 kcal; Fats: 9 g; Carbohydrates: 77 g; Protein: 21 mg

123
Vegetable and Egg Casserole

 15 minutes

 30 minutes

 4

Ingredients

- 6 eggs
- 1 cup egg whites
- 1 cup of cheese, shredded
- 16 oz. bag frozen spinach
- 2 cups mushrooms, sliced
- 1 bell pepper, diced

Directions

1. Preheat your oven to 350°F.
2. Beat the eggs with the egg whites, cheese, spinach, mushrooms, and bell pepper in a bowl.
3. Spread this egg mixture across the base of a casserole dish.
4. Bake this casserole for 30 minutes in the oven.
5. Serve warm.
6. **Serving suggestion:** Serve the casserole with cauliflower salad.
7. **Variation tip:** Top the casserole with onion slices before cooking.

Nutrition: Calories: 272 kcal; Fats: 16 g; Carbohydrates: 6 g; Protein: 26 g

124
Zesty Veggie Chicken

 10 minutes

 5 minutes

 3

Ingredients

- 1 lb. chicken tender, skinless, boneless and cut into chunks
- 10 oz. vegetables, frozen
- ⅓ cup zesty Italian dressing
- ½ tsp Italian seasoning
- 1 cup of onions, fried
- ⅔ cup of rice
- 1 cup of chicken broth
- Pepper, to taste
- Salt, to taste

Directions

1. Add all ingredients except vegetables into the Instant Pot. Meanwhile, cook frozen vegetables in the microwave according to the packet directions.
2. Seal the pot with a lid and cook on high for 5 minutes. Once done, allow the pressure to release naturally for 10 minutes then release the remaining pressure using quick release. Remove the lid.
3. Add the cooked vegetables and stir well. Serve and enjoy.

Nutrition: Calories: 279 kcal; Fats: 6.7 g; Carbohydrates: 19 g; Protein: 33 g

125
Zucchini Cream Soup

10 minutes   **40 minutes**   **3**

Ingredients

- 1 lb. zucchini, chopped
- 3 cups vegetable broth
- 1 small onion, chopped
- 2 cups milk, low-fat
- 4 tbsp Greek yogurt
- 1 tsp fresh sage, finely chopped
- 1 garlic clove, crushed
- 1 tsp olive oil
- ½ tsp salt
- ¼ tsp ground black pepper

Directions

1. Peel the zucchinis and chop them into bite-sized pieces. Set aside.
2. Peel the onion and chop it into small pieces. Set aside.
3. Preheat the oil in a heavy-bottomed pot over medium-high temperature. Add onion and garlic and stir-fry until translucent.
4. Now, add the zucchini slices and sprinkle with some sage to taste. Pour the vegetable broth and stir it all well. Bring it to a boil and then reduce the heat to low. Cover with a lid and cook for about 25–30 minutes more. Remove from the heat and set aside to cool for a while.
5. Transfer all to the food processor and blend until creamy. Now, return to the pot and heat. Sprinkle with salt and pepper and remove from the heat.
6. Stir in the Greek yogurt and milk.
7. Serve warm.

Nutrition: Calories: 182 kcal; Fats: 7.6 g; Carbohydrates: 19 g; Protein: 10 g

126
Egg Salad

10 minutes   **0 minutes**   **2**

Ingredients

- 5 hard-boiled eggs, peeled and diced
- 1 tbsp red onion, diced
- 1 green onion, sliced
- ¼ cup cucumber diced
- ¼ cup mixed olives, chopped
- ¼ cup feta cheese, crumbled
- 5 ⅓ oz. plain Greek yogurt
- ¼ cup roasted red peppers, chopped
- Salt and black pepper, to taste

Directions

1. In a salad bowl, mix the cucumber, yogurt, green onion, red onion, chopped olives, and feta.
2. Stir in the eggs and adjust the seasoning with salt and black pepper.
3. Toss in the roasted red peppers and mix evenly.
4. Serve.

Nutrition: Calories: 438 kcal; Fats: 29 g; Carbohydrates: 19 g; Protein: 28 g

127
Chickpea Curry

 15 minutes   15 minutes   3

Ingredients

- 1 (15 oz.) can of chickpeas, rinsed
- 2 (14 oz. each) cans of no-salt-added chopped tomatoes, canned and undrained
- 1 onion, chopped
- 1 serrano pepper, chopped
- 4 garlic cloves, minced
- 1-piece fresh ginger, chopped
- 6 tbsp canola oil
- 2 tsp ground coriander
- 2 tsp ground cumin
- ½ tsp ground turmeric
- 2 tsp garam masala
- Fresh cilantro, chopped, for serving (1 tbsp)

Directions

1. Put the serrano pepper, garlic, and ginger in a blender and process until minced. Add the onion and blitz until coarsely chopped.
2. Preheat canola oil in a pan over medium heat. Add the garlic and onion mixture and cook for about 3–4 minutes, stirring often.
3. Add coriander, cumin, turmeric, and garam masala, and cook for 2 minutes.
4. Add tomatoes and bring to a boil. Reduce the heat to low and cook for about 4 minutes, stirring often.
5. Add chickpeas and cook covered for 5 minutes. Serve topped with cilantro.

Nutrition: Calories: 616 kcal; Fats: 18 g; Carbohydrates: 95 g; Protein: 26 g

Chapter 4

SNACKS

128
Broccoli and Tofu Quiche

 10 min   15 min   2

Ingredients

- ¼ tsp salt
- ¼ lb. mushrooms, chopped
- 1 tbsp white miso paste
- 1-piece yellow onion, chopped
- 2 tbsp sesame tahini
- ½ cup bulgur wheat, uncooked
- 1 tbsp sesame oil
- ½ lb. broccoli, chopped
- ½ lb. tofu
- 1 tbsp tamari

Directions

1. Set the oven to 350°F
2. Fill a small pot with water (1 cup) and heat on medium. Bring to the boil before adding the bulgur and salt.
3. Stir to combine and allow the mixture to boil again. Reduce the heat to low and cover to cook for about fifteen minutes. Meanwhile, grease a pie pan (9-inch) with a little oil. Pour the cooked bulgur into the pie pan, pressing lightly to spread it evenly at the bottom. Place in the oven to bake for about twelve min or until crusty on the top. Let it stand to cool.
4. Heat a large skillet (nonstick) on medium-high before adding the onions. Stir in the mushrooms and broccoli and cook for 2 minutes. Cover and immediately remove from the heat. Meanwhile, fill the food processor with the tofu. Add the tamari, tahini, and white miso paste. Process until well-combined and smooth, then pour into a large bowl.
5. Add the cooked veggies and gently toss until evenly coated. Transfer the veggie mixture onto the crusted bulgur. Bake in the oven for about half an hour. Once done, let it stand on a wire rack. After ten minutes, slice into 6 portions and serve immediately.

Nutrition: Calories: 278 kcal; Fats: 11 g; Carbohydrates: 28g; Protein: 20.5 g

129
Artichoke Salad

10 minutes　　　　**0 minute**　　　　**2**

Ingredients

- 3 (12 oz.) jars of marinated artichoke hearts, drained
- ½ cup pitted olives, seasoned
- ½ large green pepper, chopped
- ¼ large red onion, sliced
- ½ pint cherry tomatoes
- 4 oz. feta cheese, crumbled
- 2 tbsp red wine vinegar
- ¼ cup olive oil
- 1 tbsp fresh oregano, chopped
- Zest of 1 lemon
- Salt and black pepper, to taste

Directions

1. Mix all the ingredients in a salad bowl.
2. Serve.

Nutrition: Calories: 319 kcal; Fats: 16 g; Carbohydrates: 23 g; Protein: 19 g

130
No-Bake Energy Bites

5 minutes　　　　**0 minutes**　　　　**8**

Ingredients

- 1 cup dry oatmeal
- ½ cup chocolate chips
- ½ cup peanut butter
- ½ cup smoked flaxseed
- ⅓ cup honey
- 1 tsp Vanilla

Directions

1. Mix all the ingredients and roll into balls.
2. Store in the fridge or freezer for a little treat instead of a candy bar.

Nutrition: Calories: 232 kcal; Fats: 13 g; Carbohydrates: 28 g; Protein: 5 g

131
Sweet Plums Mix

10 minutes   15 minutes   2

Ingredients

- 1 lb. plums, stones removed and halved
- 2 tbsp coconut sugar
- ½ tsp cinnamon powder
- 1 cup of water

Directions

1. In a pan, combine the plums with the sugar and the other ingredients, bring to a simmer and cook over medium heat for 15 minutes.
2. Divide into bowls and serve cold.

Nutrition: Calories: 127 kcal; Fats: 0 g; Carbohydrates: 26 g; Protein: 2 g

132
Cauliflower Hummus

6 minutes   15 minutes   6

Ingredients

- 3 cups cauliflower florets
- 3 tbsp. fresh lemon juice
- 5 cloves garlic, divided to use according to recipe instructions
- 5 tbsp. olive oil, divided to use according to recipe instructions
- 2 tbsp. water
- 1 ½ tbsp. Tahini paste
- 1 ¼ tsp salt, divided to use according to recipe instructions
- Smoked paprika and extra olive oil for serving

Directions

1. In a microwave-safe bowl, combine cauliflower, water, 2 tablespoons oil, ½ teaspoon salt, and 3 whole cloves garlic. Microwave on high 15 minutes, or until cauliflower is soft and darker in colour.
2. Transfer mixture to a food processor or blender and process until almost smooth. Add tahini paste, lemon juice, remaining garlic cloves, remaining oil, and salt. Blend until almost smooth.
3. Place the hummus in a bowl then drizzle lightly with olive oil and a sprinkle or two of paprika. Serve with your favorite raw vegetables.

Nutrition: Calories:112; Carbohydrates: 6g; Fats: 9g; Protein: 2g

133
Cheese Crisp Crackers

6 minutes

11 minutes

4

Ingredients

- 4 slices pepper Jack cheese, quartered
- 4 slices Colby Jack cheese, quartered
- 4 slices cheddar cheese, quartered

Directions

1. Heat oven to 400 degrees. Line a cooking sheet with parchment paper.
2. Place cheese in a single layer on prepared pan and bake 10 minutes, or until cheese gets firm.
3. Transfer to paper towel line surface to absorb excess oil. Let cool, cheese will crisp up more as it cools.
4. Store in airtight container, or Ziploc bag. Serve with your favorite dip or salsa.

Nutrition: Calories: 234; Carbohydrates: 1g; Protein: 17g; Fats: 18g

134
Cheesy Onion Dip

6 minutes

5 minutes

8

Ingredients

- 8 oz. low fat cream cheese, soft
- 1 cup onions, grated
- 1 cup low fat Swiss cheese, grated
- 1 cup lite mayonnaise

Directions

1. Heat oven to broil.
2. Combine all ingredients in a small casserole dish. Microwave on high, stirring every 30 seconds, until cheese is melted and Ingredients are combined.
3. Place under the broiler for 1-2 minutes 'til the top is nicely browned. Serve warm with vegetables for dipping.

Nutrition: Calories: 137; Carbohydrates: 2g; Protein: 7g; Fats: 11g

135
Cheesy Pita Crisps

6 minutes

15 minutes

8

Ingredients

- ½ cup mozzarella cheese
- ¼ cup margarine, melted
- 4 whole-wheat pita pocket halves
- 3 tbsp. reduced fat parmesan
- ½ tsp garlic powder
- ½ tsp onion powder
- ¼ tsp salt
- ¼ tsp pepper
- Nonstick cooking spray

Directions

1. Heat oven to 400 degrees. Spray a baking sheet with cooking spray.
2. Cut each pita pocket in half. Cut each half into 2 triangles. Place, rough side up, on prepared pan.
3. In a small bowl, whisk together margarine, parmesan and seasonings. Spread each triangle with margarine mixture. Sprinkle mozzarella over top.
4. Bake 12-15 minutes or until golden brown.

Nutrition: Calories: 120; Carbohydrates: 9g; Protein: 5g; Fats: 7g

136
Chili Lime Tortilla Chips

6 minutes

15 minutes

10

Ingredients

- 12 6-inch corn tortillas, cut into 8 triangles
- 3 tbsp. lime juice
- 1 tsp cumin
- 1 tsp chili powder

Directions

1. Heat oven to 350 degrees.
2. Place tortilla triangles in a single layer on a large baking sheet.
3. In a small bowl stir together spices.
4. Sprinkle half the lime juice over tortillas, followed by ½ the spice mixture. Bake 7 minutes.
5. Remove from oven and turn tortillas over. Sprinkle with remaining lime juice and spices. Bake another 8 minutes or until crisp, but not brown. Serve with your favorite salsa, serving size is 10 chips.

Nutrition: Calories:65; Carbohydrates: 12; Fats: 1g; Protein: 2g

137
Cinnamon Apple Chips

6 minutes

11 minutes

2

Ingredients

- 1 medium apple, sliced thin
- ¼ tsp cinnamon
- ¼ tsp nutmeg
- Nonstick cooking spray

Directions

1. Heat oven to 375 degrees. Spray a baking sheet with cooking spray.
2. Place apples in a mixing bowl then add spices. Toss to coat.
3. Arrange apples, in a single layer, on prepared pan. Bake 4 minutes, turn apples over and bake 4 minutes more.
4. Serve immediately or store in airtight container.

Nutrition: Calories: 36; Carbohydrates: 9g; Protein: 0g; Fats: 0g

Chapter 5
DESSERTS

138
Almond Plum Muffins

10 minutes | 25 minutes | 2

Ingredients

- 3 tbsp coconut oil, melted
- ½ cup almond milk
- 4 eggs, whisked
- 1 tsp vanilla extract
- 1 cup almond flour
- 2 tsp cinnamon powder
- ½ tsp baking powder
- 1 cup of plums, pitted and chopped

Directions

1. Pre-heat the over to 350°F
2. In a bowl, combine the coconut oil with the almond milk and other ingredients and whisk well.
3. Divide into a muffin pan and bake for 25 minutes.
4. Serve the muffins cold.

Nutrition: Calories: 550 kcal; Fats: 44 g; Carbohydrates: 19 g; Protein: 25 g

139
Banana Vanilla Cream Yogurt

5 minutes | 0 minutes | 1

Ingredients

- 1 medium banana
- 1 graham cracker
- 1 tsp fresh lemon juice
- 1 cup non-fat vanilla yogurt

Directions

1. Slice the banana into a bowl.
2. Break the graham cracker into small pieces and add to the banana.
3. Sprinkle with lemon juice and top with yogurt.

Nutrition: Calories: 265 kcal; Fats: 3 g; Carbohydrates: 55 g; Protein: 9 g

140
Dates Cream

5 minutes   0 minutes   2

Ingredients

- 1 cup almond milk
- 1 banana, peeled and sliced
- 1 tsp vanilla extract
- ½ cup coconut cream
- 1 cup of dates, chopped

Directions

1. In a blender, combine the dates with the banana and the other ingredients.
2. Pulse well, divide into small cups and serve cold.

Nutrition: Calories: 325kcal; Fats: 13 g; Carbohydrates: 53 g; Protein: 2.5 g

141
Minty Fruit Salad

5 minutes   0 minutes   2

Ingredients

- 2 cups of blueberries
- 3 tbsp mint, chopped
- 1 pear, cored and cubed
- 1 apple, cored, cubed
- 1 tbsp coconut sugar

Directions

1- In a bowl, mix the blueberries with the mint and the other ingredients, toss, and serve cold.

Nutrition: Calories: 196 kcal; Fats: 0.5 g; Carbohydrates: 55 g; Protein: 2 g

142
Mocha Chocolate Mousse

5 minutes   **0 minutes**   **2**

Ingredients

- 1 (12 oz./340 g.) package of sugar-free chocolate chips
- 1 tbsp erythritol
- 1 cup boiling black coffee
- 3 eggs
- 1 tsp vanilla

Directions

1. Combine the chocolate chips and erythritol in the blender. Turn the blender on high and slowly pour in the boiling coffee.
2. Keep the blender running and add the eggs, 1 at a time. Turn the blender to low, add the vanilla and blend for another 10 seconds.
3. Pour the mixture into 8 oz. (227 g.) glasses and set them in the freezer. You can eat this frozen, or just leave it in the freezer until it sets. Serve chilled.

Nutrition: Calories: 374 kcal; Fats: 21 g; Carbohydrates: 27 g; Protein: 11 g

143
Peanut Butter Coconut Popsicle

15 minutes   **0 minutes**   **1 - 2**

Ingredients

- ½ cup peanut butter
- 1 tsp liquid stevia
- 2 cans coconut milk, unsweetened

Directions

1. Put all the listed ingredients in a blender and blend until smooth.
2. Pour the mixture into the Popsicle molds and place in the freezer for 4 hours or until set. Serve!

Nutrition: Calories: 380 kcal; Fats: 33 g; Carbohydrates: 15 g; Protein: 13 g

144
Pumpkin Balls

 15 minutes   0 minutes   18 balls

Ingredients

- 1 cup almond butter
- 5 drops liquid stevia.
- 2 tbsp coconut flour
- 2 tbsp pumpkin puree
- 1 tsp pumpkin pie spice

Directions

1. Mix pumpkin puree in a large bowl with almond butter until well combined.
2. Add liquid stevia, pumpkin pie spice, and coconut flour and mix well.
3. Make small balls from the mixture and place them onto a baking tray in the freezer for 1 hour. Serve and enjoy.

Nutrition: Calories: 121 kcal; Fats: 8 g; Carbohydrates: 10.8 g; Protein: 5 g

145
Rhubarb Compote

 10 minutes   15 minutes   1

Ingredients

- 2 cups of rhubarb, roughly chopped
- 3 tbsp coconut sugar
- 1 tsp almond extract
- 2 cups of water

Directions

1. In a pot, combine the rhubarb with the other ingredients.
2. Toss and bring to a boil over medium heat.
3. Simmer for 15 minutes, divide into bowls and serve cold.

Nutrition: Calories: 116 kcal; Fats: 0.1 g; Carbohydrates: 27 g; Protein: 2 g

146
Strawberry Granita

 10 minutes   3 hours   3

Ingredients

- 3 cups fresh strawberries, sliced
- 1 tbsp erythritol
- ½ cup warm water
- 2 tbsp fresh lemon juice = 1 oz.

Directions

1. In a blender dissolve the erythritol with the water. Once dissolved add the strawberries and the lemon juice.
2. Puree until smooth. Pour into an 8x8 dish. Freeze for 3 hours. Stir completely.
3. Freeze for another 5 hours or overnight. Allow it to sit on the counter for around 10 minutes. Grate with the end of a fork and serve in 1 cup dishes.

Nutrition: Calories: 181 kcal; Fats: 0.3 g; Carbohydrates: 46 g; Protein: 1 g

147
Swedish Blueberry Soup

 5 minutes   8 minutes   4

Ingredients

- 3 cups (450 g) blueberries, fresh or frozen, and thawed
- 3 tbsp - ¼ cup (44 - 60 ml) maple syrup
- ½ tsp ground cardamom
- ¼ tsp ground cinnamon
- 3 tbsp lemon juice, freshly squeezed
- 2 cups (474 ml water)
- 2 tsp cornstarch or tapioca flour for paleo
- 1 tbsp cold water, optional

Directions

1. In a large, deep, non-reactive saucepan, bring the blueberries, 3 tbsp maple syrup, cardamom, cinnamon, lemon juice, and water to a boil over medium heat.
2. Let it boil for 5 minutes. Remove from the heat.
3. If you'd like the mixture to be thicker, mix the cornstarch with 1 tbsp cold water and stir it into the soup.
4. Return the pan to the heat, bring it to a boil, and then remove it from the heat.
5. Let it cool for 15–20 minutes before serving. Add the last tbsp (or more) of maple syrup, if desired. Can also be served chilled.
6. Goes well with a little Greek yogurt mixed in.
7. Refrigerate any leftovers for up to 3 days.

Nutrition: Calories: 86 kcal; Fats: 0.25 g; Carbohydrates: 23 g; Protein: 0.75 g

148
Tropical Fruit Salad

 15 minutes

 0 minutes

 2

Ingredients

- 1 cup of fresh pineapple chunks
- ½ cup of orange, chopped
- ½ cup of dried papaya, chopped
- 1 banana, sliced
- ½ cup of unsweetened, flaked coconut
- 1 cup of low-fat yogurt
- 1 medium piece of crystallized ginger, finely chopped
- 1 tsp vanilla
- A pinch of nutmeg

Directions

1. Combine all the fruit and the coconut.
2. Mix the yogurt, ginger, and vanilla and stir into the fruit.
3. Top with a pinch of nutmeg.

Nutrition: Calories: 319 kcal; Fats: 8.5 g; Carbohydrates: 53 g; Protein: 5 g

Chapter 6

4-WEEK MEAL PLAN

Week 1

Day 1
Breakfast: Blueberry Protein Pancakes **Lunch:** Bacon Jalapeño Poppers **Dinner:** Asparagus Avocado Soup
Day 2
Breakfast: Broccoli and Tofu Quiche **Lunch:** Barley and Lentil Stew **Dinner:** Vegan Edamame Quinoa Collard Wraps
Day 3
Breakfast: Cabbage and Coconut Chia Smoothie **Lunch:** Grilled Chicken Wings **Dinner:** Broccoli Gorgonzola Soup
Day 4
Breakfast: Cheese-Filled Acorn Squash **Lunch:** Cilantro Lime Shrimp with Salad **Dinner:** Chicken Bisque
Day 5
Breakfast: Heart-Friendly Sweet Potato and Oats Waffles **Lunch:** Broiled White Fish Parmesan **Dinner:** Chickpea Pepper Soup
Day 6
Breakfast: Hearty Alkaline Strawberry Summer Deluxe **Lunch:** Beef Steak Nuggets with salad **Dinner:** Creamy Leek Soup
Day 7
Breakfast: Mango Pineapple Green Smoothie **Lunch:** Lean Mean Soup **Dinner:** Marinated Tuna with salad

Week 2

Day 1
Breakfast: Mint Orange Infused Water **Lunch:** Barley and Lentil Stew **Dinner:** Chicken Casserole

Day 2
Breakfast: Raspberry Popsicle **Lunch:** Catfish with Cajun Seasoning **Dinner:** Vegetable and Egg Casserole

Day 3
Breakfast: Refreshing Strawberry Limeade **Lunch:** Herb-Roasted Pork Loin with Salad **Dinner:** Walnut and Beet Salad

Day 4
Breakfast: Sensational Strawberry Medley **Lunch:** Chipotle Shredded Pork with Salad **Dinner:** Lentils and Quinoa Stew

Day 5
Breakfast: Simple Tofu Breakfast Scramble **Lunch:** Crispy Fish Sandwich with Salad **Dinner:** Cauliflower Soup

Day 6
Breakfast: Strawberry Mint Infused Water **Lunch:** Catfish with Cajun Seasoning **Dinner:** Mom's Sloppy Joes

Day 7
Breakfast: Sweet Potato Waffles **Lunch:** Egg Casserole **Dinner:** Paprika Backed Chicken Breasts

Week 3

Day 1

Breakfast: Blueberry Multigrain Pancakes
Lunch: Chickpeas and Pumpkin Curry
Dinner: Easy Beef Kofta

Day 2

Breakfast: Baked Broccoli and Eggs
Lunch: Beef Meatballs
Dinner: Creamy Leek Soup

Day 3

Breakfast: Banana and Almond Flax Glass
Lunch: Cooked Ham Mousse
Dinner: Zucchini Cream Soup

Day 4

Breakfast: Ezekiel Bread French Toast
Lunch: Creamy Beef Stroganoff with Mushrooms
Dinner: Sushi Roll

Day 5

Breakfast: Blueberry Protein Pancakes
Lunch: Chickpea Salad
Dinner: Marinated Tuna with Salad

Day 6

Breakfast: Cinnamon Chiller
Lunch: Roast and Mushroom
Dinner: Lentils and Quinoa Stew

Day 7

Breakfast: The Mean Green Smoothie
Lunch: Fish Finger Sandwich
Dinner: Creamy Wild Asparagus Soup

CLAIM YOUR AMAZING FREE BONUS

WITH THIS QR CODE

DOWNLOAD THE FULL COLOR EDITION

WITH THIS QR CODE